funky
chunky
knitted accessories

60 ways and more to make and customize hats, bags, scarves, mittens and capelets

jan eaton

D&C
David and Charles

A DAVID & CHARLES BOOK

David & Charles is an F+W Publications
Inc. company
4700 East Galbraith Road
Cincinnati, OH 45236

First UK edition published 2006

Conceived and produced by
Breslich & Foss Ltd, London

Volume © Breslich & Foss Ltd, 2006
Text: **Jan Eaton**
Photography: **Martin Norris**
Design: **Elizabeth Healey**
Project Management: **Janet Ravenscroft**

A catalogue record for this book is available
from the British Library.

ISBN-13: 978-0-7153-2436-3
ISBN-10: 0-7153-2436-5

Printed in China by Wai Man
for David & Charles
Brunel House   Newton Abbot   Devon

Visit our website at
www.davidandcharles.co.uk

David & Charles books are available from
all good bookshops; alternatively you can
contact our Orderline on 0870 9908222 or
write to us at FREEPOST EX2 110, D&C
Direct, Newton Abbot, TQ12 4ZZ (no
stamp required UK only).

funky chunky

knitted accessories

contents

introduction

Taking a range of five easy-to-make knitting patterns as a starting point, we show you how to turn a simple accessory into something wonderfully individual. By crafting edgings and trimmings, fastenings, handles and a wide range of embellishments and combining them with chunky knitting, you can create items that are truly unique.

Begin by checking out the Basic Techniques section on pages 8 to 24. Here you'll find all the information you need to take up the craft of knitting and become proficient with yarn and needles. Each technique is presented in an easy-to-understand sequence of instructions illustrated with close-up photographs that will help you every step of the way.

Once you've become familiar with basic knitting skills, try out some of the basic patterns on pages 25 to 27. Whether you want to make a scarf, hat, bag, pair of mittens or a capelet, you'll find these basic accessories are easy to knit. If you can handle casting on, working knit stitches and casting off, you're ready to make your first scarf. As your skills and confidence improve with practice, try the basic hat and bag, then go on to make the mittens and capelet.

Delving into the next three chapters you can begin to express yourself and have some real fun! Drawing on a wealth of decorative ideas and suggestions, there are over 60 inspiring accessories based on the five basic patterns. To make it easy to find your way around the book, the designs are divided into three sections. Edgings and

Trimmings, pages 28 to 51, concentrates on different types of edgings and trimmings including fringes, pompoms, hem variations, appliqué and tassels. Fastenings and Handles, pages 52 to 75, shows you how to make and attach different styles of handles and fastenings including bag handles, ties, braids, tabs with buckles, zippers and ribbon bows. Beading and Embellishment, pages 76 to 99, goes wild with buttons, beads, bells and charms. Here you'll discover how to add glitz with beads, stitch embellishments onto your knitting, and make your own knitted buttons.

The final chapter, Customizing Knitting on pages 100 to 115 contains inspiring suggestions and helpful hints for doing something a little bit different with your knitting. This chapter shows you how to improvise your own variations of basic patterns, work with different stitch patterns and incorporate novelty yarns. It also covers getting to grips with easy washing-machine felting, working embroidery on knitting and knitting with recycled fabrics.

At the back of the book, starting on page 116, you'll find an illustrated Gallery, which contains a photograph of every accessory and variation in the book. The designs are arranged by item so that all the same accessories are shown together. Browse through the pictures and enjoy working out what to make for your next knitting project.

jan eaton

chapter 1
basic techniques and patterns

This introductory section contains everything you need to know to get started in the craft of knitting. From **choosing and handling yarns** and needles to blocking finished pieces, and from joining a new yarn to making up the accessories, all the essentials are shown here in clear step-by-step photographs. Once you have mastered the art of knitting and purling, turn to the **Basic Patterns** on page 25. Here you'll find instructions for making the **Buttonhole Bag**, **Scarf**, **Mittens**, **Hat** and **Capelet**.

Materials

A ball of chunky yarn, a pair of knitting needles, and a basic sewing kit are all you need to get started with this fascinating craft. Yarn and needles come in a variety of weights, materials and sizes: the information in this section will help you choose which to buy.

YARN

Each project in the book can be knitted with your own choice of yarn. As well as using different colours, fibre composition is also a choice you have to make. Many knitters prefer to use pure wool yarns, but there are times when synthetic yarns are preferable, particularly for items that require frequent washing. Wool yarns are also more expensive than wool/synthetic blends and those made entirely from synthetics. You may prefer to use a pure cotton or synthetic/cotton blend yarn as these are less itchy than some made from wool.

You can also be adventurous and incorporate some textured yarns, such as mohair, tweed or ribbon yarn in your accessory, but try to combine yarns of similar weight. As well as chunky weight yarns, you can use finer weights and knit with two or more strands together to make a thicker yarn. The scarf on page 110 is knit with two yarn strands; one is smooth and the other is a textured fun fur yarn.

Novelty and solid-coloured chunky weight yarns

Chunky weight yarn

Novelty ribbon yarn

Suggestions for yarn combinations

To make up a chunky yarn weight, try combining:

- Three strands of 4ply (sport weight) yarn.
- Two strands of DK (double knitting) yarn.
- One strand of Aran (worsted weight) yarn plus one of 4ply (sport weight) yarn.

Two strands of DK yarn

One strand of Aran yarn plus one strand of 4ply yarn

Three strands of 4ply yarn

NEEDLES

The basic knitting tool is a pair of needles. Single-pointed, straight knitting needles come in a range of sizes from small (2mm or US size 0) to large (15mm or US size 19) to suit different weights of yarn. Straight needles are made from aluminium, wood, bamboo or different types of plastic and they are usually available in two lengths: 25 and 36cm (10 and 14in). Choose whichever type of needle feels best in your hands and is comfortable to use.

Ball bands

The ball band – or paper tag on knitting yarn – has lots of useful information printed on it, including the fibre content of the yarn, its weight and the yardage of the ball or skein. Some bands also include suggested needle sizes and tension measurements, as well as washing or dry-cleaning information.

Useful yarn/needle combinations

4ply (sport weight) 3.25 to 3.75mm (US sizes 3 to 5)

DK (double knitting) 3.75 to 4mm (US sizes 5 to 7)

Aran (worsted weight) 4 to 5.5mm (US sizes 7 to 9)

Chunky (chunky weight) 5.5 to 8mm (US sizes 9 to 11)

KNITTING EQUIPMENT

1 Use a **row counter** to keep track of the number of rows you work.

2 Sewing **needles** with large eyes are available in a range of sizes to suit different yarn weights.

3 Use a **stitch marker** to mark your place. Split coil markers like these are better than solid rings: they can be slipped from needle to needle or attached directly into a stitch.

4 Keep one or two **crochet hooks** in different sizes handy to pick up dropped stitches.

5 Available in different shapes, **stitch holders** hold groups of stitches that will be worked later in the pattern.

6 Buy a retractable **tape measure** that has both imperial and metric measurements. Fibreglass tapes are the most accurate because they do not stretch.

7 Buy a small pair of **scissors** with sharp points. If you want to keep scissors in your knitting bag, buy a pair with a sheath or put a plastic point protector over the points.

8 Glass- or plastic-headed **pins** are easy to see and don't slip through knitted fabric. Use ordinary dressmaking pins or buy special marking ones that are longer.

9 Safety pins are invaluable for catching and holding dropped stitches before they ladder.

Optional equipment

A set of plastic pompom forms are useful for making different sizes of pompom. A wooden knitting nancy (or knitting spool) is also useful, enabling you to make tubular cords for fastening or trimming accessories. A notebook and pencil are handy for jotting down rows if you don't have a row counter. Don't put pens in your bag as they may leak and ruin your knitting and yarn.

Common knitting abbreviations

alt – alternate

beg – beginning

cont – continue

dec - decrease

foll – following

inc - increase

K – knit

K2tog – knit 2 stitches together

M1 – make 1 extra stitch

P – purl

P2tog – purl 2 stitches together

psso – pass slipped stitch over

rem – remaining

rep – repeat

RS – right side of work

sl – slip next stitch

sl 1, K1, psso – slip 1, knit 1, pass
   slipped stitch over

st(s) – stitch(es)

St st – stocking stitch

tbl – through back loops

tog – together

WS – wrong side of work

YO – yarn over needle

Holding Yarn and Needles

There is no right or wrong way to hold the yarn and needles when you are knitting: experiment until you find the most comfortable method. Some knitters control the yarn with their right hand by feeding it through and around their fingers. Others control the yarn with the left hand and hold the right needle like a pen.

Pen grip with yarn in right hand

Hold the left needle with your hand over the top and the right needle like a pen, and use your right hand to control the flow of the yarn. Use your right forefinger to make a stitch without letting the needle drop.

Pen grip with yarn in left hand

Hold the left needle with your hand over the top, using the left hand to control the yarn. Hold the right needle like a pen. Hold the yarn taut with your left hand and catch the yarn with the tip of the right needle to make a stitch.

Knife grip with yarn in right hand

Hold the left needle with your hand over the top and the right needle overhand like a knife, and use your right hand to control the flow of the yarn, taking your right hand off the needle to make a stitch. Some knitters tuck the end of the right needle under their right arm, others hold both needles with their left thumb where the points cross.

Knife grip with yarn in left-hand

Hold the left needle with your hand over the top, using the left hand to control the yarn. Hold the right needle like a knife. When making a stitch, hold the yarn taut with your left hand and catch the yarn with the tip of the right needle to make a stitch.

Starting to knit

The first step when starting to knit is to place the required number of stitches on the needle, beginning with a slip knot. This process is called casting on. There are several methods of casting on and each produces a different kind of edge.

MAKING A SLIP KNOT

Make a slip knot on the left needle to anchor the end of the yarn before casting on the required number of stitches. Make the knot with your fingers, then slip it onto the needle.

1 Pull a short length of yarn from the ball. Make a loose loop of yarn round your first finger.

2 Keeping the first loop intact, push the strand of yarn attached to the ball through the first loop to make a new loop.

3 Slip the loop off your finger. Place the new loop on the needle and tighten both ends of yarn so the loop is pulled close to the needle.

CASTING ON

The cable method is a good way to cast on as it produces a neat edge.

1 Make a slip knot and place it on one needle. Hold the needle with the knot in your left hand with the short yarn end held firmly under your fingers. Take the other needle in your right hand and insert the tip into the loop.

2 Bring the yarn from the ball over the right needle so that it is between the needle points. Use the tip of the right needle to pull a new loop of yarn through the previous loop. Then use the right needle to lift the loop onto the left needle. Tighten the yarn gently. Two stitches are now cast on.

3 Insert the right needle behind the first stitch on the left needle, wrap the yarn over and pull a new loop of yarn through onto the right needle. Place the new loop on the left needle. Repeat this step until you have the number of stitches needed on the left needle. If your cast-on stitches are very tight, it's a good idea to use a left needle one size larger when casting on. This will help prevent a tight edge to your work.

WORKING A ROW OF KNIT STITCHES

The knit stitch is one of two foundation stitches in knitting: knit and purl. When you work every row of knitting in this stitch, the resulting ridged pattern is called garter stitch and the knitted fabric looks the same on both sides. When your final pattern row has been knitted, secure the stitches by casting off as shown on page 19.

1 Hold the needle with the stitches in your left hand. Insert the tip of the right needle into the first stitch and bring the yarn over between the needles with your right hand.

2 Pull the yarn through the stitch with the right needle, and at the same time, slip the original stitch off the left needle.

3 The newly made knit stitch is on the right needle, seen in the foreground. Proceed along the row, making 1 knit stitch on the right needle from every stitch on the left needle. To work the next row, turn the work, hold the needle with the stitches in your left hand and repeat from Step 1.

Garter stitch

WORKING A ROW OF PURL STITCHES

Purl stitches are the opposite of knit stitches. The best-known combination of knit and purl stitches is called stocking stitch, which is made by knitting and purling alternate rows. Knit rows form the smooth right side of stocking stitch and the purl rows form the ridged wrong side.

1 Holding yarn and needles in the same way as for working knit stitches and with the yarn at the front of the work, insert the tip of the right needle into the front of the first stitch from right to left.

2 Loop yarn around the tip of the right needle.

3 Use the tip of the right needle to draw a loop of yarn through the stitch to make a new stitch on the right needle. Slip the old stitch off the left needle.

4 Proceed along the row, making 1 purl stitch on the right needle from every stitch on the left needle. To work the next row, turn the work, hold the needle with the stitches in your left hand and repeat from Step 1 of Knit Stitches.

Stocking stitch: right side (above) and wrong side (below)

WORKING SINGLE RIB

Simple rib patterns are combinations of knit and purl stitches arranged to make stretchy, flexible fabrics that spring back into shape when stretched. This feature makes them ideal for working hats and cuffs. Single rib (also known as 1x1 rib) alternates single knit and purl stitches along the row. It can be worked over an odd or even number of stitches. The example below is worked over 26 stitches.

1 With the yarn at the back of the work, knit the first stitch on the left needle.

2 Bring the yarn forward to the front of the work between the needles and purl the next stitch on the left needle.

3 Take the yarn to the back of the work between the needles and knit the next stitch. Continue along the row, working alternate knit and purl stitches and changing the position of the yarn after every stitch.

4 On the next and subsequent rows, as the stitches face you, knit the knit stitches and purl the purl stitches.

1

2

3

4

Single rib

WORKING DOUBLE RIB

Double rib (also known as 2x2 rib) alternates pairs of knit and purl stitches. It can be worked only over an even number of stitches. The example below is worked over 26 stitches.

1 With the yarn at the back of the work, knit the first 2 stitches on the left needle.

2 Bring the yarn forward to the front of the work between the needles and purl the next 2 stitches on the left needle.

3 Take the yarn to the back of the work between the needles and knit the next 2 stitches. Continue along the row, working alternate pairs of knit and purl stitches and changing the position of the yarn after every 2 stitches.

4 On the next and subsequent rows, as the stitches face you, knit the knit stitches and purl the purl stitches.

Double rib

WORKING MOSS STITCH

Moss stitch is a variation of single rib which makes a fairly thick fabric that lies flat and has an attractive textured surface. Moss stitch can be worked over an odd or even number of stitches and the example below is worked over 26 stitches.

1 With the yarn at the back of the work, knit the first stitch on the left needle.

2 Bring the yarn forward to the front of the work between the needles and purl the next stitch on the left needle.

3 Take the yarn to the back of the work between the needles and knit the next stitch. Continue along the row, working alternate knit and purl stitches and changing the position of the yarn after every stitch.

4 On the next and subsequent rows, as the stitches face you, knit the purl stitches and purl the knit stitches.

Moss stitch

ALL ABOUT TENSION

The term 'tension' refers to the number of stitches and rows contained in a given width and length of knit fabric. The patterns in this book include a recommended tension for the yarn that has been used and it's important that you match this tension exactly so your work comes out the right size. This is usually quoted as 'x stitches and y rows to 10cm (4in)' measured over a certain stitch pattern using a certain size of needles. Tension can be affected by the type of yarn used, the size and brand of the knitting needles and the type of stitch pattern. For items such as scarfs and bags, getting the correct tension is less important than when making mittens or hats, where a good fit is crucial.

Making and measuring a tension sample

Read the pattern instructions to find the recommended tension. Working in the exact yarn you will use for the item, make a generously sized sample 15–20cm (6–8in) wide. Work in the required pattern until the piece is 15–20cm (6–8in) long. Fasten off the yarn. Block the tension sample using the method suited to the yarn composition (page 23) and allow to dry.

1 Lay the sample right side up on a flat surface and use a ruler or tape measure to measure 10cm (4in) horizontally across a row of stitches. Mark this measurement by inserting 2 pins exactly 10cm (4in) apart. Make a note of the number of stitches (including partial stitches) between the pins. This is the number of stitches to 10cm (4in).

2 Turn the sample on its side. Working in the same way, measure 10cm (4in) across the rows, again inserting 2 pins exactly 10cm (4in) apart. Make a note of the number of rows (including partial rows) between the pins. This is the number of rows to 10cm (4in).

How to adjust the tension

If you have more stitches or rows between the pins inserted in your sample, your tension is too tight and you should make another sample using needles one size larger. If you have fewer stitches or rows between the pins, your tension is too loose and you should make another sample using needles one size smaller. Block the new sample and measure the tension as before. Repeat this process until your tension matches that given in the pattern.

JOINING A NEW YARN

When you have used up your first ball of yarn, you need to join in the next ball. Always join a new yarn at the beginning of a row to avoid holes appearing in your knitting. Use this method for joining a different colour of yarn, for example, when working a striped pattern.

1 Tie the new yarn around the end of the old yarn, using an overhand knot and leaving a tail of about 15cm (6 in).

2 Tighten the knot and push it up close to the edge of the work ready to make the first stitch of the new row.

3 Work the new row using the new ball of yarn. When the knitting is finished, undo the knot and darn in the yarn ends.

DEALING WITH YARN ENDS

Thread the end of the yarn in a large yarn needle. Weave the end through several stitches on the wrong side of the work. Trim the remaining yarn.

MAKING A BUTTONHOLE

Working a 1-row horizontal buttonhole is the neatest way to make any size of buttonhole and has the advantage of not needing any reinforcing. You can make buttonholes on either a right-side row as shown, or on a wrong-side row.

1 Work along the row to the position indicated on the pattern, bring the yarn forwards to the front of the work and slip the next stitch purlwise to the right needle without knitting it. Return the yarn to the back of the work.

2 Slip the next stitch on the left needle and pass the first slipped stitch over it and off the right needle to cast off 1 stitch.

3 Repeat Step 2 for the number of times indicated in the pattern. Here, the step has been repeated 3 times more and 4 stitches have been cast off. Slip the last cast-off stitch from the right needle back onto the left needle and turn the work.

4 Keeping the yarn at the back, cast on the number of stitches indicated in the pattern and turn. This is usually 1 more stitch than the total number of stitches cast off in Steps 2 and 3. Turn the work.

5 Keeping the yarn at the back, slip the first stitch from the left needle onto the right needle. Pass the first cast-on stitch over the slipped stitch and off the needle to close the buttonhole. Work to the end of the row.

4

4

5

1

2

3

CASTING OFF

When your final pattern row has been knitted, cast off the stitches to prevent them unravelling.

1 Knit the first 2 stitches on the left needle in the usual way. Insert the left needle into the first stitch on the right needle and lift it over the second stitch and off the needle. Knit the next stitch on the left needle and repeat until there is 1 stitch left on the right needle. Cut the yarn, leaving a 15cm (6in) tail, and pull it through the last stitch to finish.

USING A STITCH HOLDER

A stitch holder is a useful piece of knitting equipment as it lets you remove some of the working stitches from the needle and hold them safely out of the way until needed. If you don't have a stitch holder to hand, use a spare piece of yarn instead as shown in Steps 3 and 4.

1 Open the stitch holder. Slip the point of the holder into the first stitch on the left needle and carefully ease it off the needle and onto the bar of the holder.

2 Repeat Step 1 until the correct number of stitches has been transferred to the holder as shown. Close the holder so the stitches are held securely and continue knitting across the stitches still on the needle. When the stitches on the holder are needed, transfer them from the holder back onto the knitting needle in the same way.

3 When no stitch holder is available, use a length of contrasting yarn to hold the stitches. Use a yarn needle to thread the yarn through the stitches, taking them off the needle and onto the yarn one by one.

4 When the correct number of stitches has been transferred, knot the yarn ends to make a large loop. When the stitches are needed, undo the knot and carefully slip the stitches back onto the knitting needle.

WORKING INTO THE BACK OF STITCHES

The front of each stitch is always the loop closest to you on the left needle, whether you are working right- or wrong-side rows. Unless stated in the pattern instructions, always work into the front loop of the stitch. When instructed to work into the back loop, work a knit stitch as shown below.

1 To knit into the back loop of a stitch, insert the tip of the right needle under the left needle and into the loop of the stitch furthest from you.

2 Wrap the yarn over the right needle and knit this loop in the usual way, then slip it off the left needle.

SLIPPING STITCHES

Many patterns tell you to slip 1 or more stitches. This is done by passing the slipped stitches across from the left to the right needle without actually working them. Stitches can be slipped knitwise or purlwise.

1 To slip a stitch knitwise, insert the tip of the right needle into the next stitch on the left needle exactly as if you were going to knit the stitch. Pull this stitch off the left needle without knitting it. The stitch is now on the right needle.

2 To slip a stitch purlwise, insert the tip of the right needle into the next stitch on the left needle exactly as if you were going to purl the stitch. Pull this stitch off the left needle without purling it. The stitch is now on the right needle.

WORKING INCREASES AND DECREASES

Increases and decreases alter the number of stitches on the needle in any given row. They are used to shape a piece of knitting and when knitting a lace pattern. When shaping knitting, increases and decreases are usually worked 1 or 2 stitches in from the edge of the knitting rather than on the edge as this gives a neater finish.

Working a make-one increase

One extra stitch is worked into the horizontal strand of yarn between 2 ordinary knit stitches. Knit through the back loop of the strand to avoid a small hole forming and make an almost invisible increase.

1 Knit to the position of the increase. Insert the tip of the right needle from front to back into the strand of yarn between the last stitch worked and the first stitch on the left needle.

2 Using the right needle, carefully lift the strand and place it on the left needle to form a loop of yarn. Remove the right needle.

3 Knit the strand through the back loop (see page 20) and slip the loop off the left needle to leave a new stitch on the right needle. One stitch has been increased.

Working a yarn over

A yarn over is a decorative increase used in making lace patterns. It is made by wrapping the yarn around the right needle in various ways depending on where the yarn over is placed in the instructions. The simplest type of yarn over is made between 2 knit stitches on a right side row and this is the only type used in this book.

1 Work to the point indicated in the pattern. To work the yarn over, bring the yarn between the needles from back to front of the work.

2 Knit the next stitch in the usual way, taking the yarn to the back over the top of the right needle as you knit. The yarn forms an extra stitch and makes a neat eyelet hole.

3 On the next (wrong-side) row, purl the yarn overs in the same way as the ordinary stitches.

Working a basic right-slanting decrease

Knitting 2 stitches together on a right-side row is the simplest way of decreasing 1 stitch. This method of decreasing is called a single right-slanting decrease as the finished decrease slants to the right on the knit side of the work.

1 Work to the point indicated in the pattern. Insert the tip of the right needle from front to back into the next 2 stitches on the left needle as if you were going to knit.

2 Take the yarn around the needle and pull it through both stitches. Slip both stitches off the needle. One stitch has been decreased.

Working a basic left-slanting decrease

Slip 1, knit 1, pass slip stitch over is a left-slanting decrease that mirrors the slant of the knit 2 together decrease, shown left, when worked on a right-side row. For a neat finish when shaping, work a right-slanting decrease near the beginning of the row and a left-slanting decrease near the end.

1 Work to the point indicated in the pattern. Slip the next stitch from the left needle knitwise onto the right needle. Knit the next stitch in the usual way.

2 Insert the tip of the left needle into the front of the slipped stitch and lift the slipped stitch over the knit stitch and off the right needle. One stitch has been decreased.

1

2

PRESSING AND BLOCKING

Press knitting lightly on the wrong side, setting your iron temperature according to the information given on the ball band of your yarn. Avoid pressing synthetic yarns as they will become limp and lifeless – or melt – with too much heat. Press ribbed items very lightly as they may flatten and lose their stretch.

Blocking (shown below) involves pinning out knit fabric to the correct size, then either steaming it with an iron or moistening it with cold water depending on the fibre content of your yarn. Pin out your finished item to the correct size on a flat surface, such as your ironing board or a specialist blocking board using rust-proof pins. It's a good idea to block tension swatches (page 18) before measuring them.

1

1 To block woollen yarns with warm steam, hold a steam iron set at the correct temperature for the yarn about 2cm (^{3}/4in) above the surface of the knitting and allow the steam to penetrate for several seconds without allowing the iron to come into contact with the fabric. Lay the board flat and allow to dry before removing the pins.

2 To block synthetic and wool/synthetic blend yarns, pin out as above, then use a spray bottle to mist the item with clean, cold water until it is evenly moist all over, but not saturated. Pat with your hand to help the moisture penetrate more easily. Lay the board flat and allow to dry before removing the pins.

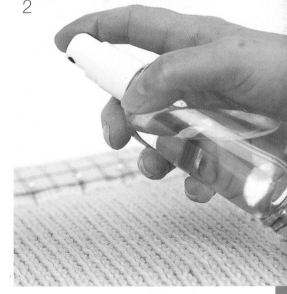

2

SEAMS

There are several methods of joining pieces of knitting. The methods shown below are both good for making up garments. Use the same yarn for both knitting and seams, unless your yarn is very thick or textured, in which case use a finer yarn of matching colour. A back stitch seam is durable and has little stretch, so use this method for seaming bags. A flat seam has more stretch and works best for seaming hats. Use either method for seaming mittens and capelets.

Flat seam

1 Pin the right sides together, inserting the pins horizontally a few stitches away from the edge. Secure the yarn by taking a few stitches over the top of the seam.

2 With your index finger between the layers, insert the needle from back to front through both layers as close to the edge as you can. Repeat along the seam.

1

Backstitch seam

1 Place the edges to be joined together with the right sides of the knitting facing each other and pin them together, inserting the pins at right angles to the edge. Thread the yarn into a needle and secure the yarn at the right edge of the seam by working 2 or 3 small stitches around the 2 edges ending with the yarn in front.

2 Insert the needle into the knitting just behind the end of the previous stitch, bringing the point through a short distance in front to make the first back stitch.

3 Put the needle back into the knitting where the previous stitch ended and make another stitch the same length as before. Repeat Step 3 along the seam, taking care not to pull the stitches too tightly.

1

2

2

3

Basic Patterns

This section contains basic patterns for a knitted bag, scarf, pair of mittens, hat and capelet. The best starting projects for a beginner are the garter stitch scarf on this page and the rib hat on page 27.

THE BASIC BAG—BUTTONHOLE BAG

YOU WILL NEED
2 100g balls of pure wool chunky yarn with approx 92m (100yds) per 100g ball

Pair of 6mm (size 10) knitting needles or size needed to achieve tension

Yarn needle

FINISHED SIZE
Bag measures 14cm (9 $^1/_2$in) deep and 29cm (11 $^1/_2$in) wide.

TENSION
15 stitches and 19 rows to 10cm (4in) over stocking stitch

KNITTING THE BAG FRONT
Cast on 42 sts.
ROW 1: (RS) Knit.
ROW 2: K1, P to last st, K1.
Rep Rows 1 & 2 until 42 rows have been worked, ending with a WS row.

Make buttonhole
BUTTONHOLE ROW: (RS) K12, bring yarn to front, slip next stitch purlwise, take yarn to back, * slip next stitch on left needle, pass first slipped stitch over it and off right needle; rep from * 17 times more (18 sts cast off). Slip last cast-off stitch on right needle to left needle and turn work. Cast on 19 sts and turn work again. With yarn at back, slip first stitch from left needle onto right needle, pass first cast-on stitch over it and off needle, knit remaining 11 sts. (42 sts)

Shape handle
ROW 1: (WS) K1, P to last st, K1.
ROW 2: Knit.
Rep Rows 1 & 2 once, then rep Row 1 once more. Cast off.

KNITTING THE BAG BACK
Work as for Front.

FINISHING THE BAG
Press pieces lightly on wrong side. Darn yarn ends on wrong side using yarn needle. Place pieces together with right sides facing and pin around edges. Using same yarn in yarn needle, back stitch down one side, across bottom and up second side. Turn bag to right side.

THE BASIC SCARF

YOU WILL NEED
2 100g balls of pure wool chunky yarn with approx 92m (100yds) per 100g ball

Pair of 6.5mm (size 10 $^1/_2$) knitting needles or size needed to achieve tension

Yarn needle

FINISHED SIZE
Scarf measures 14cm (5 $^1/_2$in) wide and 122cm (48in) long.

TENSION
15 stitches and 26 rows to 10cm (4in) measured over garter stitch.

KNITTING THE SCARF
Cast on 22 sts.
ROW 1: (WS) Knit to end.
ROW 2: (RS) Knit to end.
Using garter stitch throughout (knit every row), work until scarf is approx 122cm (48in) long, ending with a RS row.
NEXT ROW: (WS) Cast off.

FINISHING THE SCARF
Darn yarn ends on wrong side with yarn needle.

THE BASIC MITTENS

YOU WILL NEED
2 [2, 2] 100g balls of pure wool chunky yarn with approx 92m (100yds) per 100g ball

Pair of 5mm (size 8) and 5.5mm (size 9) knitting needles or sizes needed to achieve tension

Yarn needle

SIZES
To fit women's sizes Small, Medium, Large (instructions for Medium and Large sizes are given in square brackets).

SPECIAL ABBREVIATION
M1 = make an extra stitch (see page 21)

TENSION
15 stitches and 20 rows to 10cm (4in) over stocking stitch using 5.5mm (size 9) needles.

KNITTING THE RIGHT MITTEN
Using 5mm (size 8) needles, cast on 29 [33, 37] sts.

ROW 1: (RS) K1, * P1, K1; rep from * to end.
ROW 2: * P1, K1; rep from * to last st, P1.
Rep Rows 1 & 2 for 5 [5, 6] cm (2 [2, 2½] in), ending with a RS row.
NEXT ROW: Rib 6 sts, M1, (rib 4 [5, 6] sts, M1) 4 times, rib 7 sts. (34 [38, 42] sts)
Change to 5.5mm (size 9) needles and stocking stitch (RS rows knit, WS rows purl).
Beg with a knit row, work 4 [4, 6] rows of St st. **

Shape thumb gusset
ROW 1: (RS) K17 [19, 21], M1, K3, M1, K to end. (36 [40, 44] sts)
Work 3 rows of St st without shaping.
ROW 5: K17 [19, 21], M1, K5, M1, K to end. (38 [42, 46] sts)
ROW 6 and every alt row: Purl.
ROW 7: K17 [19, 21], M1, K7, M1, K to end. (40 [44, 48] sts)
Cont as set, inc 2 sts on every foll alt row until there are 44 [48, 52] sts on the needle.
NEXT ROW: Purl.

Divide for thumb
NEXT ROW: (RS) K30 [32, 34], turn.
*** NEXT ROW: P11 [13, 13], turn.
Working on these 11 [13, 13] sts only, work 8 [10, 12] rows without shaping.
NEXT ROW: K1, * K2tog; rep from * to end.(6 [7, 7] sts)
Break off yarn, leaving long tail of about 30cm (12in). Thread end into yarn needle and slot needle through remaining stitches on knitting needle. Pull yarn gently to gather stitches and slip off knitting needle. With RS facing, rejoin yarn at base of thumb and knit to end of row.
(33 [35, 39] sts)
Work 13 [15, 17] rows without shaping.

Shape top
ROW 1: (RS) K1, (sl 1, K1, psso, K11 [12, 14], K2tog, K1) twice. (29 [31, 35] sts)
ROW 2 and every alt row: Purl.
ROW 3: K1, (sl 1, K1, psso, K9 [10, 12] K2tog, K1) twice.
Cont as set, dec 4 sts on every foll alt row until there are 21 [23, 23] sts on needle, ending with a WS row. Cast off.

KNITTING THE LEFT MITTEN
Work as given for right mitten up to **.

Shape thumb gusset
ROW 1: (RS) K14 [16, 18], M1, K3, M1, K to end. (36 [40, 44] sts)
Work 3 rows of St st without shaping.
ROW 5: K14 [16, 18], M1, K5, M1, K to end. (38 [42, 46] sts)
ROW 6 and every alt row: Purl.
ROW 7: K14 [16, 18], M1, K7, M1, K to end. (40 [44, 48] sts)
Cont as set, inc 2 sts on every foll alt row until there are 44 [48, 52] sts on the needle.
NEXT ROW: Purl.

Divide for thumb
NEXT ROW: (RS) K27 [29, 31], turn.
Work as given for right mitten from ***.

FINISHING THE MITTENS
Press lightly on wrong side. Using yarn tail in yarn needle, join thumb seam using back stitch seam or flat seam. Darn yarn ends on wrong side with yarn needle. With matching yarn, join remaining seams using either back stitch seam or flat seam.

THE BASIC HAT

YOU WILL NEED

1 100g ball of pure wool chunky yarn with approx 92m (100yds) per 100g ball

Pair of 6mm (size 10) and 7mm (size 10 1/2) knitting needles or sizes needed to achieve tension

Yarn needle

FINISHED SIZE

Hat measures 20cm (8in) deep and will fit average head.

TENSION

16 stitches and 18 rows measured over double rib, slightly stretched widthways, using 6mm (size 10) needles.

KNITTING THE HAT

Using 7mm (size 10 1/2) needles, cast on 72 sts.
Change to 6mm (size 10) needles.
ROW 1: (RS) * K2, P2; rep from * to end.
Rep Row 1 until you have worked 33 rows. (72 sts)

Shape hat crown

ROW 1: (WS) * K2 tog, P2; rep from * to end. (54 sts)
ROW 2: * K2 tog, P1; rep from * to end. (36 sts)

ROWS 3 & 4: * K1, P1; rep from * to end.
ROW 5: * K2 tog; rep from * to end. (18 sts)
ROW 6: * K2 tog; rep from * to end. (9 sts)

FINISHING THE HAT

Break off yarn, leaving a long tail of about 38cm (15in). Thread end into yarn needle and slot needle through remaining stitches on knitting needle. Pull yarn gently to gather stitches and slip off knitting needle. Press hat lightly on wrong side. Using long yarn tail yarn in yarn needle, join with a flat seam. Weave in yarn end on wrong side.

THE BASIC CAPELET

YOU WILL NEED

2 100g of pure wool Icelandic Lopi yarn with approx 100m (109yds) per 100g ball

Pair of 6.5mm (size 10 1/2) knitting needles or size needed to achieve tension

Yarn needle

FINISHED SIZE

Capelet measures 18cm (7in) deep and 122cm (48in) along lower edge from front to back. Ties are 38cm (15in) long.

TENSION

13 stitches and 17 rows to 10cm (4in) measured over stocking stitch.

KNITTING THE FRONT AND HALF BACK PANELS (make two)

Cast on 75 sts and knit 5 rows.

Shape front and back edges

ROW 6: (RS) K2, sl 1, K1, psso, K67, K2tog, K2. (73 sts)
ROWS 7, 9, 11, 13, 15 & 17: K1, P to last st, K1.
ROW 8: K2, sl 1, K1, psso, K65, K2tog,

K2. (71 sts)
ROW 10: K2, sl 1, K1, psso, K63, K2tog, K2. (69 sts)
ROW 12: K2, sl 1, K1, psso, K61, K2tog, K2. (67 sts)
ROW 14: K2, sl 1, K1, psso, K59, K2tog, K2. (65 sts)
ROW 16: K2, sl 1, K1, psso, K57, K2tog, K2. (63 sts)
ROW 18: K2, sl 1, K1, psso, K55, K2tog, K2. (61 sts)
ROW 19: K1, P to last st, K1.

Shape shoulder

ROW 1: (RS) K2, sl 1, K1, psso, K23, K2tog, K3, sl 1, K1, psso, K23, K2tog, K2. (57 sts)
ROWS 2, 4, 6 & 8: K1, P to last st, K1.
ROW 3: K2, sl 1, K1, psso, K21, K2tog, K3, sl 1, K1, psso, K21, K2tog, K2. (53 sts)
ROW 5: K2, sl 1, K1, psso, K19, K2tog, K3, sl 1, K1, psso, K19, K2tog, K2. (49 sts)
ROW 7: K2, sl 1, K1, psso, K17, K2tog, K3, sl 1, K1, psso, K17, K2tog, K2. (45 sts)
ROW 9: K2, sl 1, K1, psso, K15, K2tog, K3, sl 1, K1, psso, K15, K2tog, K2.

(41 sts)
ROWS 10–12: Knit. BO.

KNITTING THE TIES (make two)

CO 45 sts. Knit 2 rows. BO.

FINISHING THE CAPELET

Press pieces lightly on wrong side. Darn yarn ends on wrong side with yarn needle. Pin 2 main pieces together with right sides facing and 2 outside edges aligning to form seam down centre back. Using same yarn in yarn needle, back stitch edges together. Pin short edge of tie to wrong side of each front edge at neckline and stitch securely to capelet.

chapter 2
edgings
and trimmings

Delightfully fluffy **pompoms**, **knotted fringes** and embroidered **appliqué** shapes are just some of the edgings and trimmings used in this chapter to transform our **five basic accessories**. Many of the projects have a **variation** that shows how the main technique can be adapted to another item. Feel free to alter the colours and designs to suit your own style and your wardrobe, or to combine the ideas here with those from other chapters. Why not add beads to the **picot hem** of the Julia mittens on page 41, for example?

Prefer the bag? **see page 25 for the basic pattern**

playful

scarf with pompoms

Pompoms are fun decorations to stitch to each corner of a plain garter stitch scarf. The secret to making a delightfully fluffy pompom is to use plenty of yarn, which can be all of one colour or a combination of several colours and types of yarn to give a multi-coloured effect.

YOU WILL NEED

- ■ 4 50g balls of pure wool double knitting yarn with approx 120m (131yds) per 50g ball
- ■ Oddments of the same yarn in 2 or 3 contrasting colours
- ■ Pair of 6.5mm (size 10½) knitting needles or size needed to achieve tension
- ■ Pompom maker or stiff card
- ■ Yarn needle

NOTE

Yarn is used double throughout. You can buy sets of adjustable plastic pompom rings or simply cut two identical doughnut shapes from sturdy card. When cutting your own shapes, make the centre ring about one quarter of the diameter of the outer ring.

FINISHED SIZE

Scarf measures 15cm (6in) wide and 122cm (48in) long

TENSION

15 stitches and 26 rows to 10cm (4in) over garter stitch, slightly stretched.

KNITTING THE SCARF

Using yarn double, knit and finish the scarf following the basic pattern on page 25.

MAKING THE POMPOMS

1 Place 2 pompom rings (or card circles) back to back. Thread several strands of yarn in yarn needle. Wind yarn around rings, adding further lengths of yarn until centre space is tightly filled.

2 Using sharp scissors, carefully cut through yarn strands, easing scissor points right between pompom rings.

3 Ease rings apart and tie length of matching yarn firmly around strands in middle of rings.

4 Pull rings apart and ease them off yarn strands. Trim off uneven pieces of yarn for a neat finish. Leave yarn ties untrimmed.

5 To attach pompoms to scarf, thread ends of yarn ties in yarn needle and stitch pompom securely in place at each corner.

1

2

4

5

pompom bag

Decorate each side of the handle of a felted Buttonhole Bag with a brightly coloured pompom made with three contrasting yarns. Thread the long ends of the ties in a yarn needle and stitch the pompoms securely in place. (See pages 112 and 113 for more on felting.)

weekend

scarf with fringe

A simple fringe makes a great finishing touch for a scarf knit in double rib. You can use the same yarn or ring the changes by adding a fringe in another colour or texture.

YOU WILL NEED

- 3 100g balls of pure wool chunky yarn with 80m (87yds) per 100g
- Pair of 6.5mm (size 10½) knitting needles or size needed to achieve tension
- Stiff card
- Large crochet hook
- Yarn needle

FINISHED SIZE

Scarf measures 15cm (6in) deep and 140cm (55in) long, not including the fringe.

TENSION

13 stitches and 18 rows to 10cm (4in) over double rib, slightly stretched widthways.

KNITTING THE SCARF

Cast on following the basic Scarf pattern on page 25.

ROW 1: (RS) * K2, P2; rep from * to last 2 sts, K2.

ROW 2: * P2, K2; rep from * to last 2 sts, P2.

Rep Rows 1 & 2 until scarf measures approximately 140cm (55in) long. Cast off.

FINISHING THE SCARF

Finish the scarf as given in the basic pattern on page 25.

Prefer the lattice scarf? **see page 25 for basic pattern**

1

2

3

4

MAKING THE FRINGE

1 Decide how deep finished fringe will be and cut rectangle of stiff card to same depth plus 2.5cm (1in). Wind yarn evenly around card and cut along bottom edge to make strands.

2 Insert large crochet hook from back to front of knitted edge. Gather desired number of strands into group, fold in half and loop fold over hook.

3 Carefully pull hook and folded yarn through to wrong side of knitting to make loop.

4 Loop hook around cut ends of yarn group and pull gently through to complete tassel. Repeat at regularly-spaced intervals along edge. Neaten by trimming any long strands.

lattice scarf

Make a knotted, lattice fringe for a more elaborate finish. Cut the strands twice as long as for a simple fringe and knot into the edge, spacing the tassels further apart. Take half the strands from one group and half the strands from an adjacent group and knot them together with an overhand knot. Repeat along the edge.

sporty

scarf with blanket stitch edging

A quick and easy embroidery edge turns a plain stocking stitch scarf into a casual yet stylish accessory. Choosing a strong colour contrast for the stitching will guarantee your handiwork stands out!

YOU WILL NEED

- 2 100g balls of pure wool chunky yarn with approx 92m (100yds) per 100g ball
- Oddments of the same yarn in a contrasting colour
- Pair of 6.5mm (size 10½) knitting needles or size needed to achieve tension
- Yarn needle

FINISHED SIZE

Scarf measures 15cm (6in) wide and 203cm (80in) long.

TENSION

14 stitches and 18 rows to 10cm (4in) over stocking stitch.

KNITTING THE SCARF

Cast on following the basic Scarf pattern on page 25.

ROW 1: (RS) Knit.

ROW 2: K1, P to last st, K1.

Rep Rows 1 & 2 until the scarf is approximately 203cm (80in) long, ending with a WS row. Cast off.

Darn in the yarn ends and press lightly on the wrong side.

WORKING THE BLANKET STITCH EDGING

1 Thread contrasting yarn in yarn needle. Begin stitching at centre of 1 long side. Insert needle into knitting about 5cm (2in) from edge and leave tail of yarn on surface. Bring needle back through knitting close to edge so it is ready to begin stitching. Tail will be secured after length of yarn has been used.

2 Take needle through knitting from front to back about 1.5cm (³⁄₄in) from edge and same distance to right from point where yarn emerged along edge. Take working thread under point of needle.

3 Carefully pull needle and yarn through to complete first blanket stitch. Repeat along edge, making evenly spaced stitches, until last stitch is worked about 1.5cm (³⁄₄in) from corner.

4 To make a neat corner, work 1 blanket stitch diagonally across corner so it shares same hole as previous stitch. To complete corner, make another blanket stitch to share same hole, working it down adjacent side of scarf.

5 To finish off yarn ends, take them through to wrong side and darn in as neatly as possible close to edge of knitting, then trim.

> **Tip**
>
> Choose a novelty yarn to work the blanket stitches. Ribbon and tape yarns work well for embroidery, but avoid eyelash yarns and those that are heavily textured.

curly

bag with curly fringe

Knitted fringes are fun to work, and this one creates wonderful corkscrew curls. Use a length of matching fringe to decorate the lower edge of a plain buttonhole bag or a garter stitch scarf.

YOU WILL NEED

■ 2 100g balls of pure wool chunky yarn with approx 92m (100yds) per 100g ball

■ Pair of 5.5mm (size 9) and 6mm (size 10) knitting needles or size needed to achieve tension

■ Sewing thread and sewing needle

■ Yarn needle

FINISHED SIZE

Bag measures 36cm (14in) deep, including fringe, and 29cm (11¹/₂in) wide.

TENSION

15 stitches and 19 rows to 10cm (4in) over stocking stitch using 6mm (size 10) needles.

KNITTING THE BAG

Knit the back and front of the bag with the 6mm (size 10) needles following the basic pattern on page 25.

FRINGE PATTERN

Using 5.5mm (size 9) needles, cast on 20 sts.

ROW 1: (RS) Cast on 15 sts, K4.

ROW 2: K5.

ROW 3: Cast on 15 sts.

Rep Rows 1 to 3 for length required, ending with a Row 1. Cast off.

Prefer the scarf? **see page 25 for the basic pattern**

KNITTING THE FRINGE

1 Cast on 20 stitches. Cast off 15 stitches to leave 4 stitches on left needle and 1 stitch on right needle.

2 Knit remaining 4 stitches. There are now 5 stitches on needle. Turn work and knit 5 stitches.

3 Turn work and cast on 15 stitches. There are now 20 stitches on needle.

4 Repeat Steps 1 to 3 to make strip of fringe long enough to fit across bottom of bag. End by casting off 15 stitches as if you were working Row 1 of pattern. Cast off remaining stitches.

5 Position fringe on right side of bag front with right sides facing, aligning lower edge of bag with top edge of fringe. Tack in place with sewing cotton.

FINISHING THE BAG

Finish the bag as described in the basic pattern, making sure you place the right sides of both front and back pieces together so the fringe is sandwiched between them.

kinky scarf

Liven up the basic Scarf by knitting two short lengths of curly fringe and stitching them across each end. You can use matching yarn as shown, or choose one of contrasting weight and texture.

violet

felted bag with fabric binding

Add a touch of colour and pattern to a plain felted bag by binding the top edge with a bias strip made from printed cotton dress fabric.

YOU WILL NEED

- 2 100g balls of pure wool Icelandic Lopi yarn with approx 100m (109yds) per 100g ball
- Pair of 7.5mm (size 10½) knitting needles or size needed to achieve tension
- Oddments of printed cotton fabric to tone with yarn
- Matching sewing thread and sewing needle
- Yarn needle

FINISHED SIZE

Bag measures 23cm (9in) deep and 30cm (12in) wide after felting.

TENSION

Working to an exact tension is not necessary when making a felted bag. Knit a tension swatch using the stated needles and machine wash it at 60°. The knit fabric should feel thick and substantial and have lost most of the stitch definition, but still be pliable. You may need to knit several swatches using different needle sizes to get a felted fabric that feels right. There's more information about felting on pages 112 and 113.

KNITTING THE BAG

Knit the bag front following the basic pattern on page 25, but do not cast off.

NEXT ROW: (RS) K1, P to last st, K1.
NEXT ROW: Knit. Cast off. Repeat for bag back.

FINISHING THE BAG

Finish the bag as described in the basic pattern, omitting pressing. Machine wash the bag at 60° and spin dry. Pull the bag gently into shape and lay flat until completely dry.

Prefer the scarf? **see page 25 for the basic pattern**

APPLYING THE BINDING

1 Fold oddment of cotton fabric across diagonal and press fold. Mark out several 4cm (1½in) strips across fabric following line of fold. Cut along lines through both layers of fabric.

2 Place ends of 2 strips with right sides together and back stitch across, close to edge. Join several strips in same way to make length that will go around top of bag, plus overlap of about 2.5cm (1in). Press strip, pressing seams open.

3 Cut ends of strip square. Fold strip along length with wrong sides together and press fold. To finish making binding, turn a narrow hem along both long edges and tack to secure.

4 Turning under raw edges at each end of binding, pin binding around top of bag to enclose bag edge, overlapping ends of strip by about 1cm (½in). Stitch binding in place on right side of bag with neat stitches and matching thread, then repeat on wrong side. Remove tacking.

bound scarf

A fabric binding makes a pretty edge on the basic Scarf. Make the binding as narrow or as wide as you like.

julia

mittens with picot hem

Instead of knitting an ordinary single or double rib cuff on your winter mittens, add a pretty picot hem. The decoration is easy to work and adds a dressy look to plain mittens.

WORKING THE PICOT HEM

1 Begin picot row by knitting first 2 stitches with 5mm (size 8) needles. Bring yarn forwards between needles, insert right needle into both of next 2 stitches, take yarn over needle and knit 2 stitches together. Continue along row alternating working 1 yarn over with knitting 2 stitches together.

2 Change to 5.5mm (size 9) needles and work next row, purling knit stitches and yarn overs made on previous row.

3 With right sides together, sew mitten seams. Fold hem to wrong side so fold runs across picot row and pin in place, inserting pins at right angles to hem.

4 Using same yarn, carefully stitch hem to mitten. Turn mitten to right side and lightly press hem with a warm iron.

YOU WILL NEED

- 2 [2, 2] 100g balls of pure wool chunky yarn with approx 92m (100yds) per 100g ball
- Pair of 5mm (size 8) and 5.5mm (size 9) knitting needles or size needed to achieve tension
- Yarn needle

FINISHED SIZES

To fit women's sizes Small, Medium, Large (instructions for Medium and Large sizes are given in square brackets).

TENSION

15 stitches and 20 rows to 10cm (4in) over stocking stitch using 5.5mm (size 9) needles.

KNITTING THE MITTENS

Using 5mm (size 8) needles, cast on 34 [38, 42] sts.

ROWS 1 & 3: (RS) Knit.

ROWS 2 & 4: Purl.

ROW 5: (RS, picot row) K2, * YO, K2tog; rep from * to end.

Change to 5.5mm (size 9) needles.

Beg with a purl (WS) row, work 9 [9, 11] rows in St st.

Change to following basic pattern on page 26, working from 'Shape thumb gusset' to end.

meadow

bag with felt appliqué flowers

Stitching bold felt shapes onto a plain stocking stitch bag is a quick way to turn it into something special. If you don't want to stitch the shapes down, use fabric glue or fusible bonding web to secure them.

YOU WILL NEED

- 2 100g balls of pure wool chunky yarn with approx 92m (100yds) per 100g ball
- Pair of 6mm (size 10) knitting needles or size needed to achieve tension
- Thin card
- Oddments of yellow and red felt
- Yellow and green embroidery floss
- Crewel embroidery needle
- Yarn needle

FINISHED SIZE

Bag measures 24cm (9¹/₂in) deep and 29cm (11¹/₂in) wide.

TENSION

15 stitches and 19 rows to 10cm (4in) over stocking stitch.

KNITTING THE BAG

Knit the back and front of the bag following the basic pattern on page 25.

Prefer the mittens? see page 26 for the basic pattern

1

2

3

4

1 Using photograph as guide to shape, draw outline of simple flower on piece of card. Cut out flower to make template. Make template for flower centre in same way by drawing around a coin or bottle top.

2 Lay flower template on yellow felt and draw around it with fine felt pen. Repeat twice more. Do same with flower centre template on red felt. Using sharp pair of scissors, cut out flowers and centres.

3 Position flowers in row along base of bag and pin in place. Using 3 strands of yellow embroidery floss, stitch flowers onto knitting with blanket stitch (page 115).

4 Pin centre on each flower. Using 3 strands of green embroidery floss, stitch flower centres down with straight stitches going across edge of felt.

dotty mittens

Decorate a pair of basic Mittens with bright spots of colour stitched down with straight stitches worked in a contrasting colour of embroidery floss.

paris

rib hat with French knit trim

You may remember making lengths of French (or spool) knitting when you were a child. Traditionally, the circular knitted cord was worked over four small nails attached to a wooden cotton reel, but today you can buy a ready-made knitting nancy (or spool), which is easier to use.

YOU WILL NEED

- 1 100g ball of pure wool chunky yarn with approx 92m (100yds) per 100g
- Oddment of double knitting yarn in a contrasting colour
- Pair of 6mm (size 10) and 7mm (size 10¹/₂) knitting needles or size needed to achieve tension
- Knitting nancy (or knitting spool)
- Yarn needle

FINISHED SIZE

Hat measures 20cm (8in) deep and will fit average head.

TENSION

16 stitches and 18 rows to 10cm (4in) over double rib, slightly stretched widthways, using 6mm (size 10) needles.

KNITTING THE HAT

Knit the hat following the basic pattern on page 27.

Prefer the scarf? **see page 25 for basic pattern**

MAKING THE CORD

1 Thread end of yarn down knitting nancy until it emerges from bottom. Wind yarn end around little finger to keep it taut and stop it slipping.

2 Keeping yarn end tensioned, wrap yarn coming from ball around each nail anti-clockwise and pull taut.

3 Lay yarn over first wrap on nail. Lift wrap over yarn and off nail using yarn needle. Work each stitch in this way, pulling yarn at bottom of nancy to keep it tensioned, until cord is 40cm (16in) long.

4 To cast off, move last knitted stitch to nail at its left. Lift bottom stitch over top stitch. Repeat until 1 stitch remains, then fasten off yarn.

FINISHING THE HAT

Finish the hat as described in the basic pattern on page 27. Darn the yarn ends of the cord, then tie a knot at each end. Using the photograph as a guide, wind the cord to make a pleasing shape and pin in place. Stitch to the hat using the cord yarn.

loopy scarf

To jazz up the basic Scarf, add several loops of contrasting French knit cord along the ends. Stitch each loop securely in place using matching yarn.

jaunty

rib hat with turn-back cuff

The classic ribbed hat looks good when a deep, turn-back cuff is added. Knit the hat in single or double rib using a solid yarn colour or vary the effect by choosing a funky, variegated yarn.

MAKING THE CUFF AND FINISHING THE HAT

YOU WILL NEED

- 1 100g ball of pure wool chunky yarn with approx 92m (100yds) per 100g
- Pair of 6mm (size 10) and 6.5mm (size 10½) knitting needles or size needed to achieve tension
- Stitch markers or oddments of contrasting yarn
- Yarn needle

FINISHED SIZE

Hat measures 20cm (8in) deep and will fit average head.

TENSION

16 stitches and 18 rows to 10cm (4in) over single rib, slightly stretched widthways, using 6mm (size 10) needles.

KNITTING THE HAT

Cast on with 6.5mm (size 10½) needles following the basic pattern on page 27.

ROW 1: (RS of cuff, WS of hat) * K1, P1; rep from * to end.

Rep Row 1 until you have worked 13 more rows, ending with a WS row.

(72 sts)

Mark each end of row with a stitch marker or piece of spare yarn.

Change to 6mm (size 10) needles.

Cont to work even in single rib, rep Row 1 until you have worked 29 more rows, ending with a RS row. (72 sts)

SHAPE CROWN OF HAT

ROW 1: (WS) K1, * K2 tog, P1, K1; rep from * to last 3 sts, K2tog, P1. (54 sts)

ROW 2: * K1, K2 tog; rep from * to end. (36 sts)

ROWS 3 & 4: * P1, K1; rep from * to end.

ROW 5: * P2 tog; rep from * to end. (18 sts)

ROW 6: * K2 tog; rep from * to end. (9 sts)

Break off yarn, leaving tail of about 20cm (8in). Thread end into yarn needle and slot needle through remaining stitches on knitting needle. Pull yarn gently to gather stitches and slip off needle. Darn in yarn end. Finish hat as shown at right.

1 Cast on required number of stitches with 6.5mm (size 10½) needles, leaving tail of yarn at beginning, 38cm (15in) long. Tail will be used to sew cuff.

2 Work 14 rows of single rib as instructed, ending with wrong side row. With right side of work facing you, mark each end of Row 14 with stitch marker.

3 If you don't have stitch markers handy, cut 2 20cm (8in) lengths of contrasting yarn. Use yarn needle to insert length of contrasting yarn at each end of row, then knot yarn ends securely.

4 Follow pattern instructions and complete hat. With wrong sides of cuff facing, use yarn tail to stitch cuff seam about 1cm (½in) beyond markers. With wrong sides of hat facing, complete hat seam.

5 Turn cuff to right side along Row 14. Working from right side of cuff, catch edge of cuff to hat with a few stitches worked into seam.

swinger

rib hat with tassel

One huge, generous tassel decorates this double rib hat. Making tassels is a great way to use up odd lengths of yarn from your collection. Mini tassels look cute added to mittens.

YOU WILL NEED

- 1 100g ball of pure wool chunky yarn with approx 92m (100yds) per 100g
- Oddments of 3 co-ordinating chunky yarns
- Pair of 6mm (size 10) and 7mm (size 10½) knitting needles or size needed to achieve tension
- Stiff card
- Yarn needle

FINISHED SIZE

Hat measures 20cm (8in) deep and will fit average head. Tassel measures 15cm (6in) long.

TENSION

16 stitches and 18 rows to 10cm (4in) over double rib, slightly stretched widthways, using 6mm (size 10) needles.

KNITTING THE HAT

Knit and finish the hat following the basic pattern on page 27.

Prefer the mittens? see page 26 for the basic pattern

MAKING THE TASSEL

1 Decide how long you want finished tassel to be and cut rectangle of stiff card to same depth plus 2.5cm (1in). Using all 4 colours together, wind yarn evenly around card 5 or 6 times, starting and ending along bottom edge of card.

2 Pass short length of main yarn under strands at top of card and knot ends tightly together. Cut strands along bottom edge of card where you began winding.

3 Holding strands together in group close to knot, wrap length of main yarn tightly around top of strands about 1cm (¹/₂in) from knot.

4 Secure end of yarn by threading it in yarn needle and taking it down through centre of wraps.

5 Trim ends of tassel neatly. Thread length of yarn knotted around top of tassel into yarn needle, pull through top of hat to wrong side and secure with several stitches

1

2

3

4

5

tasselled mittens

For a fun finish, add several tiny matching tassels to the cuff edge of a pair of basic Mittens. These tassels are made from 12 strands of chunky yarn.

swansdown

capelet with marabou trim

Wear this delightfully feminine capelet over a floaty summer dress and fasten it with ribbon ties (see Bluebell, page 74) or use a glamorous, sparkly pin or clasp.

YOU WILL NEED

- 3 50g balls of pure wool double knitting yarn with approx 120m (131yds) per 50g ball
- Pair of 6mm (size 10) and 6.5mm (size 10½) knitting needles or size needed to achieve tension
- 2.75m (3yds) of marabou trim
- Sewing thread to match yarn
- Sewing needle
- Yarn needle

NOTE

Yarn is used double throughout.

FINISHED SIZE

Capelet measures 15cm (6in) deep and 107cm (42in) along lower edge from front to back.

TENSION

15 stitches and 20 rows to 10cm (4in) over stocking stitch using 6mm (size 10) needles.

KNITTING THE CAPELET

Using yarn double, knit and finish the capelet following the basic pattern on page 27, omitting the ties.

2

3

4

APPLYING MARABOU TRIM

1 Pin marabou trim around capelet on right side, starting at centre back seam of lower edge and inserting pins at right angles to edge of knitting.

2 At corner, allow for a little extra trim to go around angle, making sure trim lies flat in wear.

3 Continue pinning trim around capelet in same way until you reach starting point, then overlap ends of trim by about 2cm (³/₄in).

4 Stitch trim down by sewing core of it carefully to right side of knitting using sewing thread that matches yarn colour. Take stitches through trim from back of knitting at right angles to core, pulling feathers free when making each stitch. Secure thread ends neatly on wrong side.

fluffy bag

Marabou trim adds a touch of glamour to a plain grey Buttonhole Bag. Position the marabou along the bottom edge, as shown, or take it up the sides as well for a bolder effect.

chapter 3
fastenings
and handles

Chapter 3 contains over a dozen fabulous ideas for using a wide range of both **handmade** and shop-bought handles and fastenings. Knitted, tied ends transform a plain scarf into an Octopus scarf that you might like to combine with the bag with **knotted** handles. Felted **drawstring** handles make a fun closure for a chunky felted bag. Divine, **sparkly buttons** make pretty fastenings for our Loopy mittens, while the basic capelet is turned into an elegant Bluebell wrap on page 74 thanks to the addition of lengths of **satin ribbon**.

tuck

scarf with slit closure

This project makes use of two shades of closely toned yarn, but there's no reason why you shouldn't combine two strongly contrasting colours for a dynamic effect. To wear the scarf, tuck the plain end through the slit.

YOU WILL NEED

- 4 50g balls of pure wool double knitting yarn with approx 120m (131yds) per 50g ball; 2 balls in main colour and 2 balls in contrasting colour
- Pair of 5.5mm (size 9) knitting needles or size needed to achieve tension
- 2 stitch holders
- Yarn needle

NOTE

One strand of main yarn and one strand of contrasting yarn are used together throughout.

FINISHED SIZE

Scarf measures 14cm (5¹/₂in) wide and 100cm (39in) long.

TENSION

17 stitches and 26 rows to 10cm (4in) over garter stitch, slightly stretched.

KNITTING THE SCARF

Holding both yarns together, cast on with 5.5mm (size 9) needles following the basic pattern on page 25.
Work in garter stitch for 15cm (6in), ending with a WS row.

* DIVIDE FOR SLIT OPENING

NEXT ROW: K11, slip rem 11 sts onto stitch holder, turn.
Work in garter stitch on these 11 sts for 10cm (4in), ending with a WS row. Put these 11 sts onto second stitch holder and break yarn, leaving tail to weave in.
NEXT ROW: With RS facing, slip sts from first holder onto needle. Rejoin yarn and work on these 11 sts in garter stitch for 10cm (4in), ending with a WS row. Break yarn, leaving tail to weave in.
Slip sts from second holder onto needle and knit across all 22 sts.
** Work even in garter stitch for 29¹/₂ in. (75 cm). Cast off.

1

2

3

4

MAKING THE SLIT

1 Work scarf up to * in pattern instructions (left), ending with wrong side row. Knit first 11 stitches on needle, then slip remaining 11 stitches onto stitch holder. Turn work and knit 10cm (4in) of garter stitch on 11 stitches on needle, ending with wrong side row.

2 Slip stitches from needle onto second holder and break off yarn. Return stitches on first holder to needle. With right side facing, rejoin yarn and knit in garter stitch for 10cm (4in), ending with wrong side row. Break off yarn.

3 With wrong side of both strips facing you, return stitches on second holder to needle. There are now 22 stitches on needle.

4 With right side of scarf facing, rejoin yarn at side edge and knit across all 22 stitches on needle. Work even in garter stitch, following pattern instructions from **.

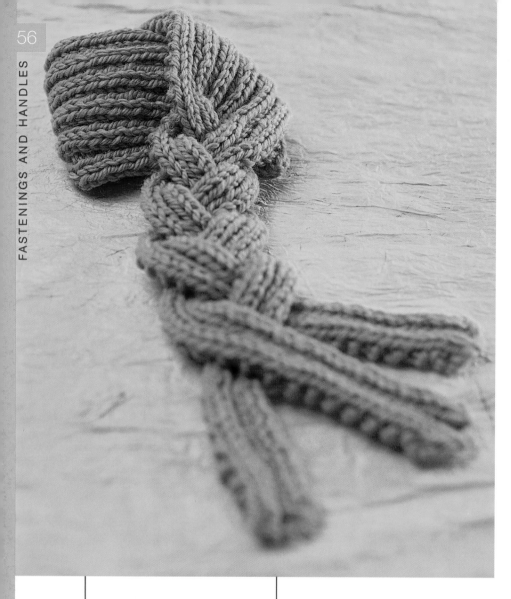

TENSION

22 stitches and 18 rows to 10cm (4in) over double rib, slightly stretched.

KNITTING THE SCARF

MAKE BEGINNING TIES

Cast on 8 sts.

ROW 1: (RS) K3, P2, K3.

** ROW 2: K1, P2, K2, P2, K1.

Rep Rows 1 & 2 28 times more, then rep Row 1 once more ***.

Make 3 ties, putting the first 2 ties onto stitch holders and leaving the last tie on the needle.

With WS of all the ties facing, slip the first 2 ties back onto the needle. (24 sts)

WORK BODY OF SCARF

FIRST ROW: **** (WS) K1, * P2, K2; rep from * to last 3 sts, P2, K1.

NEXT ROW: K3, * P2, K2; rep from * to last 5 sts, P 2, K3.

Rep these 2 rows until scarf measures approximately 107cm (42in) from ends of ties, ending with a WS row.

DIVIDE FOR THE END TIES

NEXT ROW: (RS) K3, P2, K3.

Slip rem 16 sts onto holder.

Working on 8 sts on needle, complete first tie by working from ** to ***, then cast off.

Transfer next 8 sts from holder to needle, rejoin yarn with RS facing and work to match first tie.

Transfer rem 8 sts from holder to needle and work to match first tie.

octopus

scarf with tie ends

There are lots of ways to wear the Octopus scarf. Wind it around your neck and leave the tie ends hanging loose, plait them together, or knot them in a variety of combinations.

YOU WILL NEED

- 2 100g balls of pure wool chunky yarn with approx 92m (100yds) per 100g ball
- Pair of 6.5mm (size 10$\frac{1}{2}$) knitting needles or size needed to achieve tension
- 2 stitch holders
- Yarn needle

FINISHED SIZE

Scarf measures 10cm (4in) wide and 140cm (55in) long, including ties.

Prefer the bag? see page 25 for the basic pattern

1

2

3

MAKING THE TIES

1 Make 3 identical ties as given in pattern instructions (left), breaking off yarn after knitting each one. Slip first and second ties onto stitch holders once completed, but leave third tie on knitting needle.

2 Turn needle so wrong side of third tie is facing you and transfer other 2 ties from stitch holders to same needle, making sure all ties face same way.

3 Once all 3 ties are on needle, rejoin yarn and work body of scarf from **** in pattern instructions, ending with wrong side row.

4 To make second set of ties, work across first 8 stitches on left needle in pattern and slip remaining 16 stitches onto holder. Complete first tie over 8 stitches as instructed.

5 Transfer next 8 stitches from holder to needle, rejoin yarn and work second tie to match first. Repeat with remaining 8 stitches to make third tie.

4

5

knotty bag

Use the basic Buttonhole Bag pattern, omitting the buttonhole, and make a tie on each piece like this: cast off 30 sts along the top edge to leave 12 sts on the needle. Rib 70 rows (RS rows: K3, P2, K2, P2, K3; WS rows: K1, * P2, K2; rep from * once again, P2, K1) and cast off. Stitch the bag pieces together and knot the ties to make a handle.

tab

scarf with tab-and-buckle fastening

This short scarf fastens with an ingenious knitted tab decorated with a buckle. To wear, tuck the plain end of the scarf behind the tab and adjust it to get a snug fit around your neck.

YOU WILL NEED

- 2 100g balls of pure wool chunky yarn with approx 92m (100yds) per 100g ball
- Oddments of the same yarn in a contrasting colour
- Pair of 5mm (size 8) and 6.5mm (size 10½) knitting needles or size needed to achieve tension
- Slot-through buckle about 4cm (1½in) in diameter
- Yarn needle

FINISHED SIZE

Scarf measures 15cm (6in) wide and 100cm (39in) long.

TENSION

14 stitches and 25 rows to 10cm (4in) over garter stitch using 6.5mm (size 10½) needles, slightly stretched.

KNITTING THE SCARF

Knit and finish the scarf following the basic pattern on page 25, making it approximately 100cm (39in) long. Make the tab fastening in contrasting yarn as described opposite.

MAKING THE TAB FASTENING

1 With contrasting yarn and 5mm (size 8) needles, cast on 7 stitches, leaving long yarn tail. Work in moss stitch (page 17) until tab is slightly longer than width of scarf. Cast off, leaving long yarn tail.

2 Slot buckle onto right side of tab and ease it into centre of tab.

3 Mark position of tab on right side of scarf with 2 pins, positioning them about 15cm (6in) from end of scarf.

4 Using yarn tails, stitch ends of tab to edges of scarf.

buckled bag

Two tabs with buckles make a stylish fastening for the plain Buttonhole Bag. Stitch the cast-off end of the tabs to the cast-off edge of the bag back. Secure the buckled end of the tabs with a touch-and-close strip or poppers stitched onto the back of the tabs and front of the bag.

kate

bag with grab handles

This sturdy, garter stitch bag can be knit in wool or cotton yarn and will stretch to hold a surprising amount. In the variation opposite, the basic pattern is transformed again into a handy shoulder bag.

YOU WILL NEED

- 2 100g balls of pure wool chunky yarn with approx 92m (100yds) per 100g ball
- Oddment of the same yarn in a contrasting colour
- Pair of 5.5mm (size 9) and 6mm (size 10) knitting needles or size needed to achieve tension
- Sewing thread and sewing needle
- Yarn needle

FINISHED SIZE

Bag measures 23cm (9in) deep, not including handles, and 27cm (10$\frac{1}{2}$in) wide

TENSION

15 stitches and 26 rows to 10cm (4in) over garter stitch using 6mm (size 10) needles

KNITTING THE BAG

Cast on with 6mm (size 10) needles following the basic pattern on page 25. Work the back and front in garter stitch for 66 rows, omitting the buttonhole and ending with a WS row. Cast off.

Tip

Moss stitch makes good, strong handles that keep their shape. Other suitable handle stitches are single rib (page 16) and double moss stitch, used in the Shoulder Bag variation.

Prefer the shoulder bag? **see page 25 for the basic pattern**

MAKING THE HANDLES

1 With contrasting yarn and 5.5mm (size 9) needles, cast on 5 stitches, leaving long yarn tail. Work in moss stitch until strip measures 25cm (10in) ending with right side row. Cast off, leaving long yarn tail. Make second handle to match first.

2 Mark position of handles on bag front. Insert 2 pins, each about 8cm (3in) away from side edges. Pins mark outer edge of handle.

3 Pin ends of handle to bag front, making sure cast-off edge of front overlaps handle ends slightly, and outer edges of handle align with pins.

4 Using yarn tails, back stitch ends of handle to bag front by sewing through bag below cast-off stitches. Work 2 or 3 rows of stitches to make sure handle is firmly fixed. Repeat to match on bag back.

shoulder bag

Knit the basic Buttonhole Bag pattern in stocking stitch, omitting the buttonhole row. Make a shoulder strap like this: Cast on 9 sts and work 115cm (45in) in double moss stitch (ROWS 1 & 3: * K1, P1; rep from * to last st, K1. ROWS 2 & 4: P1, * K1, P1; rep to end. Repeat Rows 1 to 4). Cast off. Overlap ends of strap and seam of RS of bag for 2.5cm (1in) and stitch securely in place.

susie

felted bag with drawstring handles

This felted bag is the perfect size for holding keys, mobile phone, purse, cosmetics and other essentials. The drawstring handles hold the top of the bag closed and are long enough to slip comfortably over a shoulder.

YOU WILL NEED

- 2 100g balls of pure wool chunky tweed yarn with approx 100m (109yds) per 100g ball
- 1 50g ball of variegated handspun Aran weight yarn in a contrasting colour with approx 100m (109yds) per 50g ball
- Pair of 7.5mm (size 10½) knitting needles or size needed to achieve tension
- Large wooden knitting needle with sharp point
- Knitting nancy (or knitting spool)
- Yarn needle

FINISHED SIZE

Bag measures 23cm (9in) deep and 30cm (12in) wide after felting.

TENSION

Working to an exact tension is not necessary when making a felted bag. Knit a tension swatch using the stated needles and machine wash it at 60°. The knit fabric should feel thick and substantial

and have lost some stitch definition, but still be pliable. You may need to knit several swatches using different needle sizes to get a felted fabric that feels right. There's more information about felting on pages 112 and 113.

KNITTING THE BAG

Knit the bag following the basic pattern on page 25, omitting the buttonhole.

KNITTING THE HANDLES

Using the contrasting yarn, make a length of French knitting 2m (78in) long following the instructions on page 45.

FINISHING THE BAG

Finish the bag as described in the basic pattern, omitting pressing. Machine wash the bag and handle at 60° and spin dry. Pull gently into shape and lay flat until completely dry.

Prefer the mittens? see page 26 for the basic pattern

ATTACHING THE HANDLES

1 Fold large inverted pleat at one side of top of bag.

2 Force wooden knitting needle through layers of pleat to make hole right through bag. Repeat Steps 1 and 2 at other side of bag.

3 Fold handle in half and cut in two. Slot first handle through holes in front of bag, leaving ends hanging in pleat at side. Slot other handle through holes in back of bag in same way.

4 Knot handle ends securely together at sides of bag. Pull handles to draw bag up so knots are hidden in pleats.

pompom mittens

Slot lengths of French knit cords through a pair of basic Mittens, just above the ribbed cuffs. Decorate the ends of the cord with contrasting pompoms made following the instructions on page 31, and tie the cord ends in bows.

honey

bag with tortoiseshell handles

There is a wide range of ready-made bag handles available in many different finishes. Faux tortoiseshell handles work well with this bag, but it would look equally attractive with bamboo or painted wooden handles.

YOU WILL NEED

- 4 50g balls of novelty felt finish chunky yarn with approx 50m (55yds) per 100g ball
- Pair of 6.5mm (size 10¹/₂) knitting needles or size needed to achieve tension
- Pair of oval faux tortoiseshell bag handles
- Tapestry wool to match yarn
- Yarn needle

FINISHED SIZE

Bag measures 28cm (11in) deep, not including handles, and 34cm (13¹/₂ in) wide.

TENSION

12 stitches and 24 rows to 10cm (4in) over garter stitch.

KNITTING THE BAG

Cast on with 6.5mm (size 10¹/₂) needles following the basic pattern on page 25. Work the back and front in garter stitch for 56 rows, omitting the buttonhole and ending with a WS row.

SHAPE TOP

** Cast off 8 sts, knit to end of row. (34 sts)

Turn, cast off 8 sts purlwise, knit to end of row. (26 sts)

DECREASE ROW: (RS) * K2tog, K1; rep to last 2 sts, K2tog. (17 sts)

*** Working on these 17 sts, knit 9 more rows without shaping, ending with a WS row. Cast off.

FINISHING THE BAG

Finish the bag as described in the basic pattern.

APPLYING THE HANDLES

1 Work bag up to ** in pattern instructions (left), ending with wrong side row. Cast off 8 stitches at beginning of next row. Knit to end of row and turn.

2 Cast off 8 stitches at beginning of next row, but this time purl the stitches you are casting off instead of knitting them. Knit to end of row. There are now 26 stitches on needle.

3 Reduce number of stitches on needle to 17 by working knit 2 together, knit 1 alternatively until last 2 stitches are reached. Knit these 2 stitches together, then follow pattern instructions from ***.

4 To attach handles, fold top of bag over handle and wrong side of knitting. Pin in place.

5 Using matching, tapestry yarn, stitch cast-off edge of bag in place with small stitches. Fasten off yarn ends securely to prevent stitches unravelling.

1

2

3

4

5

loopy

mittens with loop-and-button fastening

A series of stitched loops makes a lovely fastening for an accessory. Make the loops in matching yarn and choose pretty, ball-shaped buttons with a shank on the back to hold them above the loops.

YOU WILL NEED

- 2 [2, 3] 50g balls of pure wool double knitting yarn with approx 120m (131yds) per 50g ball
- Pair of 5mm (size 8) and 5.5mm (size 9) knitting needles or size needed to achieve tension
- 6 decorative ball buttons with shank
- Yarn needle

NOTE

Yarn is used double throughout.

FINISHED SIZES

To fit women's sizes Small, Medium, Large (instructions for Medium and Large sizes are given in square brackets).

TENSION

15 stitches and 20 rows to 10cm (4in) over stocking stitch using 5.5mm (size 9) needles.

KNITTING THE MITTENS

Using the yarn double, knit the mittens following the basic pattern on page 26. Join the mitten seams, omitting the cuff seam.

Prefer the scarf? **see page 25 for the basic pattern**

MAKING THE BUTTON LOOPS

1 Join single length of yarn at cast-on edge on back of mitten and make stitch into edge about 1cm (¹/₂in) away. Tighten yarn to leave loop around finger. Loop should be slightly larger than button so button can pass easily through it.

2 Work 2 or 3 more loops in same section of cuff, ending with yarn at left-hand edge of loops. Take small stitch through edge of knitting to secure loops.

3 Work series of blanket stitches (page 115) over yarn loops, working stitches close together so loops are completely covered with stitching.

4 Repeat along cuff to make 3 loops. Sew buttons onto opposite side of cuff to match loops.

buttoned scarf

Make a pair of button loops along one edge of a short garter stitch Scarf. Sew large decorative buttons with shanks on the opposite edge of the scarf, then fasten to make a cosy muffler.

zippy

shortie mittens with zip

A matching zip makes a neat, unobtrusive fastening for mittens. Knit an ordinary rib cuff and insert the zip into the seam, or make a shortie version as shown.

YOU WILL NEED

- 1 [1, 2] 100g balls of pure wool chunky yarn with approx 92m (100yds) per 100g ball
- Pair of 5mm (size 8) and 5.5mm (size 9) knitting needles or size needed to achieve tension
- Two 10cm (4in) lightweight zips to match yarn
- Matching embroidery floss
- Crewel embroidery needle
- Yarn needle

FINISHED SIZES

To fit women's sizes Small, Medium, Large (instructions for Medium and Large sizes are given in square brackets).

TENSION

15 stitches and 20 rows to 10cm (4in) over stocking stitch using 5.5mm (size 9) needles.

KNITTING THE MITTENS

Using 5mm (size 8) needles, cast on 34 [38, 42] sts.

ROWS 1 & 3: (RS) * K2, P2; rep from * to last 2 sts, K2.

ROWS 2 & 4: K1, P1, * K2, P2; rep from * to last 4 sts, K2, P1, K1.

Change to 5.5mm (size 9) needles.

Beg with a knit (RS) row, work 2 [2, 4] rows in St st.

Change to following the basic pattern on page 26, working from 'Shape thumb gusset' to end.

Prefer the bag? **see page 25 for the basic pattern**

APPLYING THE ZIP

1

2

3

1 Join thumb seam of mitten, then join side seam, leaving 10cm (4in) opening at base of seam to accommodate zip.

2 Turn mitten to right side. With zip pull at cuff edge, pin one side of zip to edge of opening, folding end of tape beyond pull to wrong side. Repeat, pinning other side of zip to opposite side of opening.

3 Using 2 strands of matching embroidery floss in crewel needle, back stitch zip in place along both sides of opening.

zipped bag

Add a zipped pocket to the front of the Buttonhole Bag. Omit the buttonhole and add tie handles from page 57. Knit a moss stitch pocket in two pieces, making a shallow piece for the top and a deeper piece for the base. Stitch the cast-off edges together at the sides, leaving a long opening between the pieces, and insert a matching zip in the opening. Stitch all four edges of the pocket to the bag.

TENSION

16 stitches and 22 rows to 10cm (4in) over stocking stitch using 6mm (size 10) needles.

KNITTING THE HAT

Knit and finish the hat following the basic pattern on page 27, changing to stocking stitch to work the rest of the hat after the first 4 rows of double rib have been worked.

EARFLAPS (make two)

Cast on 14 sts using 5mm (size 8) needles.

Work 14 rows in garter stitch.

** DECREASE ROW: (RS) Knit to last 3 sts, K2tog, K1.

Rep decrease row until 3 sts rem, ending with a RS row.

CORD ROW 1: (WS) K1, P1, K1.

CORD ROW 2: K3.

Rep these 2 rows until cord is approximately 30cm (12in) long, ending with a WS row.

NEXT ROW: K2tog, K1. (2 sts)

NEXT ROW: K2tog.

Fasten off yarn.

anna

hat with earflaps and cords

This hat is great fun to wear. Leave the earflaps and cords loose, tie the cords together under your chin to keep your ears warm, or knot them on top of your head to make a traditional deerstalker hat!

YOU WILL NEED:

- 2 100g balls of pure wool chunky yarn with approx 92m (100yds per 100g
- Pair of 5mm (size 8), 6mm (size 10) and 7mm (size 10¹/₂) knitting needles or size needed to achieve tension
- Crochet hook
- Yarn needle

FINISHED SIZE

Hat measures 20cm (8 in) deep and will fit average head. Earflaps and cords measure 38cm (15in) long, not including tassels.

Tip

To make the hat more colourful, use contrasting yarns in different colours to knit each earflap, then change the yarn colour again to knit the cords. Add contrasting yarn to the tassels.

Prefer the bag? see page 25 for the basic pattern

MAKING THE EARFLAPS

1 Work earflap up to ** in pattern instructions (left), ending with wrong side row. Shape earflap by knitting to last 3 stitches, knitting next 2 stitches together and knitting last stitch. Do this on every row until 3 stitches remain on needle.

2 Make cord by repeating both cord pattern rows until row measures 30cm (12in) long.

3 To shape end of cord, knit first 2 stitches together and knit last stitch. On next row, knit remaining 2 stitches together and fasten off yarn by pulling it through remaining stitch.

4 Cut 3 or 4 lengths of yarn and loop them through end of cord with crochet hook. Adjust lengths so yarn ends are level.

5 Tie yarn in overhand knot, making sure knot rests against end of cord. Trim yarn ends neatly.

ATTACHING THE EARFLAPS
Pin earlaps to each side of the hat. Try on the hat in front of a mirror and adjust the position of the earflaps if necessary. Using a flat seam, stitch the earflaps to the cast-on edge of the hat.

buttoned bag

Make a flap fastening for the Buttonhole Bag by working an earflap with a 6.5cm (2½in) cord, leaving a long yarn tail. Fold the cord in half to make a loop and wrap the tail around the cord four or five times to secure the loop. Fasten off the yarn end on the back of the flap. Stitch the flap to the back of the bag, centring it on the buttonhole. Stitch a button on the front of the bag to correspond with the loop.

heidi

rib hat with braided ties

Lengths of yarn from the same colour palette are combined to make these simple braided ties. You can make the ties wider by adding more lengths of yarn to the hat before you start plaiting.

YOU WILL NEED

- 1 100g ball of pure wool chunky yarn with approx 92m (100yds) per 100g
- Oddments of co-ordinating double knitting or worsted weight yarns
- Pair of 6mm (size 10) and 7mm (size 10½) knitting needles or size needed to achieve tension
- Yarn needle

FINISHED SIZE

Hat measures 20cm (8in) deep and will fit average head, braids measure 28cm (11in) long).

TENSION

16 stitches and 18 rows to 10cm (4in) over double rib, slightly stretched widthways, using 6mm (size 10) needles.

KNITTING THE HAT

Knit and finish the hat following the basic pattern on page 27.

MAKING THE BRAIDS

1 Mark position of braid at each side of hat with loop of yarn. Cut nine 1m (39in) lengths of different yarns for each braid. Thread braid lengths through hat at marked point, using yarn needle to thread 3 lengths through at a time.

2 When all strands have been threaded through, adjust so ends are level. Divide braid strands with your fingers into 3 groups of 6 strands.

3 Plait strands together, working at alternate sides and moving each outside group of strands into centre of braid. Continue until braid is about 25cm (10in) long.

4 Tie end of braid in overhand knot, making sure knot rests against end of braid. Trim ends neatly to make tassel.

Tip

Combining mohair, ribbon, metallic and highly textured yarns with several strands of the hat yarn will make fat, chunky braids.

Prefer the scarf? **see page 25 for the basic pattern**

braided scarf

Add braids to corners of the basic garter stitch Scarf, mixing light and dark shades of scarf colour. Wear the scarf with braids hanging loose or knot them together in pairs or in a group of four.

bluebell

capelet with ribbon ties

This plain capelet is trimmed with narrow ribs along the top and bottom edges and will sit snugly around your shoulders. It fastens with a generous bow of matching double satin ribbon.

YOU WILL NEED

- 3 100g balls of pure wool chunky yarn with 80m (87yds) per 100g
- Pair of 6.5mm (size 10¹/₂) knitting needles or size needed to acieve gauge
- 152cm (60in) of 4cm (1¹/₂in) wide matching satin ribbon
- Matching sewing thread and sewing needle
- Yarn needle

FINISHED SIZE

Capelet measures 20cm (8in) deep and 122cm (48in) along lower edge from front to back. Ties are 71cm (28in) long.

TENSION

13 stitches and 18 rows to 10cm (4in) over stocking stitch.

KNITTING THE FRONT & HALF BACK PANELS (make two)

Cast on following the basic pattern on page 27.

ROWS 1, 3 & 5: * K1, P1; rep to last st, K1.

ROWS 2 & 4: * P1, K1; rep from * to last st, P1.

SHAPE BACK AND FRONT EDGES

Work Rows 6 to 19 as given in the basic pattern.

SHAPE SHOULDER

Work Rows 1 to 9 as given in the basic pattern.

ROW 10: * K1, P1; rep to last st, K1.

ROW 11: * P1, K1; rep to last st, P1.

ROW 12: * K1, P1; rep to last st, K1.

Cast off.

FINISHING THE CAPELET

Finish the capelet as described in the basic pattern, omitting the ties.

ATTACHING THE RIBBON TIES

1 Cut ribbon into 2 equal pieces. Fold over 1cm (¹/₂in) of raw edge onto right side at 1 short end of ribbon, then fold over again to make double hem that folds onto right side of ribbon.

2 Pin hem in place then secure by stitching across folded edge using matching sewing thread.

3 Pin right side of hemmed end of tie to wrong side of each front edge at neckline overlapping them so hem on ribbon is hidden. Use matching thread to stitch securely to capelet.

4 Using sharp scissors, cut other end of ties on diagonal to make neat points.

chapter 4
beading and embellishment

Our five **funky accessories** lend themselves well to the addition of a little glitz and glamour. From silver and gold **pebble** beads to delicate **pearl** buttons, the potential for adding decorative details to the basic patterns is endless. In this section, beads are both attached to the surface of finished accessories and knitted in. **Glass cube** beads look fabulous arranged in **spiral shapes** on a felted buttonhole bag, while **chunky beads** make a fun finish for a fringed scarf. In Pearl, mother-of-pearl buttons transform a plain bag into a purse to die for. But this chapter is not just about buttons and beads: turn to page 88 for our **slashed felted bag** and scarf.

BEADING AND EMBELLISHMENT

swirl

scarf with beaded spirals

Freely worked spiral shapes made from tiny beads are randomly
scattered across the ends of this plain scarf. Combine several
colours of beads in each spiral or work them in a single colour.

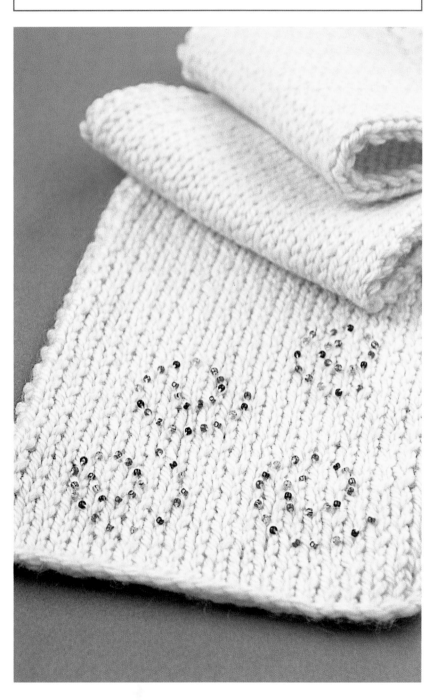

YOU WILL NEED

- 2 100g balls of pure wool chunky yarn with approx 92m (100yds) per 100g ball
- Pair of 6.5mm (size 10¹/₂) knitting needles or size needed to achieve tension
- Embroidery thread in the yarn colour
- Small glass rocaille beads in 4 contrasting colours
- Crewel embroidery needle
- Yarn needle

FINISHED SIZE

Scarf measures 15cm (6 in) wide and 178cm (70in) long.

TENSION

14 stitches and 18 rows to 10cm (4in) over stocking stitch.

KNITTING THE SCARF

Cast on following the basic pattern on page 25.

ROW 1: (RS) Knit.

ROW 2: K1, P to last st, K1.

Rep Rows 1 & 2 until the scarf is approximately 178cm (70in) long, ending with a WS row. Cast off.

Darn in the yarn ends and press lightly on the wrong side.

Cut several 1m (39in) lengths of matching embroidery floss and divide each piece of floss into single strands of thread. Fold the strand in half and insert the cut ends through the crewel needle. Use the loop method shown on page 87 to secure the thread on the wrong side of the scarf.

Prefer the bag? **see page 25 for the basic pattern**

BEADING THE SPIRALS

1 Begin at centre of spiral. Bring needle through scarf, slot green bead onto thread so it rests on knitting. Take stitch through knitting, bringing needle through short distance in front of bead. Make sure needle comes through knitted stitch, not through hole between stitches.

2 Slot orange bead onto thread so it rests on knitting. Take stitch through knitting back towards previous bead, bringing the needle through in front of orange bead.

3 Working in curved line, attach blue bead then red bead to complete colour sequence.

4 Continue to attach beads in curved line, working outwards from centre of spiral and following same colour sequence. To finish spiral, take thread through to wrong side and secure by working a few stitches into back of knitting. Work 3 or 4 spirals at each end of scarf.

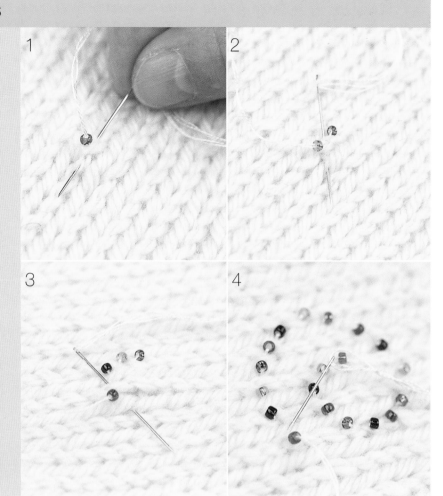

spiral bag

Felted knitting and shiny beads have attractively contrasting textures. Combine felted Icelandic wool with spirals of iridescent glass cube beads to make this pretty and unusual bag. (See pages 112 to 113 for more on felting.)

firefly

scarf with knitted-in beads

Chunky beads with a metallic finish sparkle against a dark background colour. The beads are knitted in as you go, so make sure you thread them onto the yarn before starting to knit.

WORKING THE BEADING

1 Thread 20 beads individually onto each ball of yarn using suitable size of needle. Push beads down yarn for several yards to leave enough yarn to cast on and work first few rows of pattern.

2 If beads have holes that are too small to accommodate yarn thickness, thread them onto loop of finer yarn. Loop bead and knitting yarn together as shown, then slide beads from bead yarn onto knitting yarn and move down yarn as above.

3 Following pattern instructions, knit to position of first bead. Bring yarn between needles to front of work and slip first bead down yarn so it rests snugly against knitting.

4 Slip next stitch purlwise and, holding bead at front of work, move yarn to back of work and knit to position of next bead. Repeat Steps 3 and 4 along row.

5 On next row, purl slipped stitches as usual, taking care beads do not slip through to wrong side of knitting.

FINISHING THE SCARF

Darn the yarn ends on the wrong side. Block if necessary using the cold water method on page 23.

YOU WILL NEED

- 2 100g balls of pure wool chunky yarn with approx 92m (100yds) per 100g ball
- Pair of 6mm (size 10) knitting needles or size needed to achieve tension
- 40 chunky metallic beads with hole large enough to accommodate yarn
- Yarn needle

FINISHED SIZE

Scarf measures 15cm (6in) wide and 122cm (48in) long.

TENSION

15 stitches and 24 rows to 10cm (4in) over pattern.

SPECIAL ABBREVIATION FOR THIS PATTERN

B = apply bead.

PREPARING THE YARN

Before starting to knit, thread 20 beads onto each ball of yarn.

KNITTING THE SCARF

Cast on following the basic pattern on page 25, but using 6mm (size 10) needles.

WORK BEADED BORDER

** ROW 1: (RS, ridge row) K1, P to last st, K1.

ROWS 2, 4 & 6: Rep Row 1.

ROW 3: Knit.

ROW 5: (bead row) K3, B, *K4, B; rep from * to last 3 sts, K3.

ROW 6: K1, P to last st, K1.

Rep Rows 1 to 6 four times more, ending with a Row 6 ***.

WORK SECTION WITHOUT BEADS

ROW 1: (RS, ridge row) K1, P to last st, K1.

ROWS 2, 4 & 6: Rep Row 1.

ROWS 3 & 5: Knit.

ROW 6: K1, P to last st, K1.

Rep Rows 1 to 6 thirty times more, ending with a Row 6.

WORK BEADED BORDER

Rep from ** to ***.

NEXT ROW: (ridge row) K1, P to last st, K1. Cast off.

1

2

3

4

5

charming

scarf with charms and bells

Glass and plastic heart charms are randomly scattered across the ends of a plain scarf to make a deep border. Combine the hearts with tiny gold- and silver-coloured bells to finish the decoration.

YOU WILL NEED

- 2 100g balls of pure wool chunky yarn with approx 92m (100yds) per 100g ball
- Pair of 6.5mm (size 10½) knitting needles or size needed to achieve tension
- Embroidery thread in the yarn colour
- Selection of glass and plastic heart charms and tiny metal bells
- Crewel embroidery needle
- Yarn needle

FINISHED SIZE

Scarf measures 15cm (6in) wide and 178cm (70in) long.

TENSION

14 stitches and 18 rows to 10cm (4in) over stocking stitch.

KNITTING THE SCARF

Cast on following the basic pattern on page 25.

ROW 1: (RS) Knit.

ROW 2: K1, P to last st, K1.

Rep Rows 1 & 2 until the scarf is approximately 178cm (70in) long, ending with a WS row. Cast off.

Darn in the yarn ends and press lightly on the wrong side.

Cut several 50cm (20in) lengths of matching embroidery floss and divide each piece of floss into single strands of thread. Fold the strand in half and insert the cut ends through the crewel needle. Use the loop method shown on page 87 to secure the thread on the wrong side of the scarf.

Prefer the hat? see page 27 for the basic pattern

APPLYING THE CHARMS AND BELLS

1 Attach heart charms with vertical hole through centre by working 2 or 3 long vertical stitches down hole and through scarf. Secure thread on wrong side after attaching each heart.

2 Attach heart charms with 2 or more holes through edge by working 2 or 3 stitches down through hole and through scarf. Secure each piece of thread on wrong side.

3 Attach heart charms with loop by working 2 or 3 stitches through hole and into scarf. Secure each piece of thread on wrong side.

4 Scatter hearts at random in band across each end of scarf. To finish, sew some small bells between hearts securing each bell with several stitches through loop and into scarf.

shamrock hat

Originally made to embellish cross stitch embroidery, metal charms come in a variety of shapes and finishes. Shamrock charms make the perfect decoration for the cuff of the Jaunty hat from page 46.

Tip

Beading and embroidery stores have dazzling arrays of embellishments with which to adorn your knitting. Choose lightweight charms so your knitting doesn't pull out of shape.

flora

bag with knitted ball buttons

Turn large round beads into funky buttons by covering each one with a strip of knitting. Arrange the buttons to make a flower shape to liven up the front of a plain shoulder bag.

buttoned mittens

Cover beads with strips knit with variegated yarn and use them to decorate plain Mittens. Group three buttons above the rib cuff or arrange several in a line down the back of the mitten in the same way as the shank buttons on page 92.

Prefer the mitterns? **see page 26 for the basic pattern**

YOU WILL NEED

- 2 100g balls of pure wool chunky yarn with approx 92m (100yds) per 100g ball
- Pair of 3.75mm (size 5) and 6mm (size 10) knitting needles or size needed to achieve tension
- Oddments of contrasting double knitting yarn in 2 colours
- 7 lightweight wooden or plastic beads, approximately 2mm (³/₄ in) in diameter
- Yarn needle

FINISHED SIZE

Bag measures 24cm (9¹/₂in) deep and 29cm (11¹/₂in) wide, not including strap.

TENSION

15 stitches and 19 rows to 10cm (4in) over stocking stitch using 6mm (size 10) needles.

KNITTING THE BAG

Using 6mm (size 10) needles, knit the back and front of the bag following the basic pattern on page 25, omitting the buttonhole. Make the strap by following the instructions for the Shoulder Bag variation on page 61.

MAKING KNITTED BUTTONS

1 Cast on 6 stitches on 3.75mm (size 5) needles using contrast double knitting weight yarn. Work about 10 rows of stocking stitch or until strip fits snugly around bead. Cast off. Make 6 strips in first colour and 1 strip in second colour.

2 To make each button, wrap knitted strip around bead. Using 1 of yarn tails, sew cast-on edge of strip to cast-off edge.

3 Holding bead in position, use same yarn tail to stitch from side to side of strip so it covers 1 side of bead. Secure yarn tail by slotting it through knitting and bringing it out in centre of seam.

4 Turn bead over and use remaining yarn tail to stitch strip over other side of bead. Secure this yarn tail in same way as above. Using photograph as guide to position, use yarn tails to stitch buttons to front of bag.

pearl

bag with mother-of-pearl buttons

Pearl buttons make a fantastic embellishment for a plain stocking stitch bag worked in a dark yarn colour. If you're buying the buttons, choose a variety of shapes and sizes for maximum impact or mix new and vintage buttons.

YOU WILL NEED

- 2 100g balls of pure wool chunky yarn with approx 92m (100yds) per 100g ball
- Pair of 6mm (size 10) knitting needles or size needed to achieve tension
- Selection of pearl buttons in different shapes and sizes
- Embroidery thread in bright colours
- Crewel embroidery needle
- Yarn needle

FINISHED SIZE

Bag measures 24cm (9$^{1}/_{2}$in) deep and 29cm (11$^{1}/_{2}$in) wide.

TENSION

15 stitches and 19 rows to 10cm (4in) over stocking stitch.

KNITTING THE BAG

Knit the back and front of the bag following the basic pattern on page 25.

DECORATING THE BAG

1 Cut several 50cm (20in) lengths of brightly coloured embroidery floss. Using your fingers, carefully divide each piece of floss into 3 equal sections, each containing 2 strands of thread.

2 Use 1 section of thread at a time. Fold thread in half and insert cut ends through crewel needle. On right side of bag front, take needle under knit stitch and pull thread through to leave short loop on surface.

3 Take needle through loop and pull thread gently to lock thread in place. Slot button onto thread and take it down thread to rest flat on knitting.

4 Take stitch over centre of button, going back through second hole in button and right through knitting. Bring needle through first hole and make several more stitches until button is secure, then take needle through to wrong side and work 2 or 3 stitches through knitting at back of button to secure end.

5 Repeat Steps 2 to 4 to secure each button, mixing sizes and shapes of buttons and varying thread colours. Scatter buttons at random across bag front, keeping them below buttonhole.

jenny

slashed felted bag

Contrasting handles and a decoratively slashed pocket add unique touches to this felted bag. The matching scarf is both ususual and practical: it will keep you warm and is guaranteed not to fray.

YOU WILL NEED

- 2 100g balls of pure wool chunky tweed yarn with approx 100m (109yds) per 100g ball
- Pair of 6mm (size 10) and 7.5mm (size 10½) knitting needles or size needed to achieve tension
- Oddment of variegated handspun Aran weight yarn in a similar colourway to the main yarn
- Oddment of pure wool chunky yarn in solid colour to match 1 of the colours in the variegated yarn
- Embroidery thread to match main yarn
- Crewel embroidery needle
- Yarn needle

FINISHED SIZE

Bag measures 24cm (9½in) deep, not including handles, and 29cm (11½in) wide.

TENSION

Working to an exact tension is not necessary when making a felted bag. Knit a tension swatch using the stated needles and machine wash it at 60°. The knit fabric should feel thick and substantial and have lost some stitch definition, but still be pliable. You may need to knit several swatches using different needle sizes to get a felted fabric that feels right. There's more information about felting on pages 112 and 113.

KNITTING THE BAG

Using the 7.5mm (size 10½) needles, knit and finish the bag following the basic pattern on page 25, omitting the buttonhole.

KNITTING THE POCKET

Using 6mm (size 10) needles and the solid colour yarn, cast on 28 sts.
ROW 1: (RS) Knit.
ROW 2: K1, P to last st, K1.
Rep Rows 1 & 2 fourteen more times, ending with a WS row.
Break yarn, join in contrasting variegated yarn and rep Rows 1 & 2 twice more. Cast off.

KNITTING THE HANDLES
(make two)

Using 6mm (size 10) needles and the contrasting variegated yarn, cast on 6 sts. Work 120 rows of garter stitch. Cast off.

FINISHING THE BAG

Finish the bag as described in the basic pattern, omitting pressing. Machine wash the bag and handles at 60° and spin dry. Pull gently into shape and lay flat until completely dry. Repeat with the pocket, but this time use a warm wash.

slashed scarf

Knit the basic Scarf in stocking stitch and machine wash it at 60°. Pull it into shape and allow to dry. Cut a series of 2.5cm (1in) slashes all around the edge of the scarf, then machine wash again at the same temperature to open up the slashes.

Prefer the scarf? see page 25 for the basic pattern

FINISHING THE POCKET

1 After pocket has dried, cut series of 2.5cm (1in) slashes into knitting along lower edge and both side edges. Felt pocket for second time by machine washing it on 60° wash. Ease it into shape and allow to dry.

2 Pin handles to top of bag, positioning end 5cm (2in) of handles on right side of bag. Stitch securely to bag using embroidery floss.

3 Pin pocket to front of bag, positioning pins along top edge and inside slashes on other 3 sides.

4 Using same embroidery floss, work row of large back stitches around 3 sides of pocket, positioning row of stitching a short distance inside slashes.

astra

mittens with starburst sequins

Sequins add instant glitz to the simplest of knitted accessories. Stitch them onto knitting with embroidery floss, arranging the sequins to make a pretty starburst pattern.

YOU WILL NEED

- 2 [2, 2] 100g balls of pure wool chunky yarn with approx 92m (100yds) per 100g ball
- Pair of 5mm (size 8) and 5.5mm (size 9) knitting needles or size needed to achieve tension
- Selection of cup-shaped large sequins in a variety of colours
- Embroidery thread to match 1 of the sequin colours
- Crewel embroidery needle
- Yarn needle

FINISHED SIZES

To fit women's sizes Small, Medium, Large (instructions for Medium and Large sizes are given in square brackets).

TENSION

15 stitches and 20 rows to 10cm (4in) over stocking stitch using 5.5mm (size 9) needles.

KNITTING THE MITTENS

Using 5mm (size 8) needles, cast on 34 [38, 42] sts.

ROWS 1, 3 & 5: (RS) Knit.

ROWS 2 & 4: K1, P to last st, K1.

ROWS 6, 7 & 8: Knit.

Change to 5.5mm (size 9) needles and stocking stitch.

Beg with a knit (RS) row, work 4 [4, 6] rows of St st.

Change to following the basic Mitten pattern on page 26, working from 'Shape thumb gusset' to end.

APPLYING THE SEQUINS

1 Cut 50cm (20in) length of embroidery floss and divide it into 3 equal sections. Thread cut ends of 1 section through crewel needle. On right side of back of 1 mitten, take needle under knit stitch and lock thread in place using loop method shown on page 87.

2 Slot sequin onto thread with concave side facing upwards. Take sequin down thread so it rests on knitting.

3 Take stitch over sequin, going through knitting at edge of sequin and bringing needle through short distance away at edge of sequin.

4 Work several straight stitches over sequin, working from outside and going down through hole each time, so stitches radiate from centre. Take needle through to wrong side and secure thread by working several stitches into knitting behind sequin. Repeat Steps 2 to 4 to secure each sequin, scattering them randomly across back of each mitten.

FINISHING THE MITTENS

Finish the mittens as described in the basic pattern, omitting the pressing as this may damage the sequins.

froggy

mittens with novelty buttons

A row of cartoon buttons looks bright and cheerful arranged in a line down the back of plain stocking stitch mittens. Choose buttons with shanks, rather than the sew-through type, as these will stand up nicely off the knitted fabric.

Tip

Use pearl or rhinestone buttons to decorate dressy mittens. Select buttons with fairly flat shanks so they sit on the surface and don't poke through to the wrong side.

YOU WILL NEED

- 2 [2, 2] 100g balls of pure wool chunky yarn with approx 92m (100yds) per 100g ball
- Pair of 5mm (size 8) and 5.5mm (size 9) knitting needles or size needed to achieve tension
- Oddment of contrasting yarn
- 10 novelty buttons with shanks
- Embroidery thread to match main yarn colour
- Crewel embroidery needle
- Yarn needle

FINISHED SIZES

To fit women's sizes Small, Medium, Large (instructions for Medium and Large sizes are given in square brackets).

TENSION

15 stitches and 20 rows to 10cm (4in) over stocking stitch using 5.5mm (size 9) needles.

KNITTING THE MITTENS

Knit the mittens following the basic pattern on page 26.

Prefer the hat? **see page 27 for the basic pattern**

APPLYING THE BUTTONS

1 Thread length of contrasting yarn into yarn needle. Count stitches across back of mitten and use yarn to mark centre of back by working line of large running stitches through centre stitches. Mark position of buttons with pins, spacing them evenly in a row down knitting, following line of contrast stitching.

2 Cut 50cm (20in) length of embroidery thread, divide into 2-strand sections and use loop method (page 87) to attach 1 section to position marked by pin. Remove pin, carefully snip contrast yarn and ease ends out of knitting using yarn needle.

3 Slot button onto thread, sliding it down thread to rest against knitting. Take several stitches over button shank and through knitting to fix in place.

4 Bring needle back through fabric close to shank, then wind thread 2 or 3 times around stitches beneath shank. Take needle back through to wrong side and secure thread by working several stitches into knitting behind button. Repeat Steps 2 to 4 to secure remaining buttons.

FINISHING THE MITTENS

Finish the mittens as described in the basic pattern, omitting the pressing as this may damage the buttons.

fishy hat

Tiny shank buttons look great dotted over the basic Hat knit in double rib. Match the embroidery thread colour to that of the yarn and use a separate length to stitch each button in place.

gretchen

hat with beaded ties

It's quick and easy to add simple beaded ties to hats and other accessories. Use chunky plastic craft beads to decorate the ties. They are lightweight, unbreakable and come in a wide range of colours.

YOU WILL NEED

- 2 100g balls of pure wool chunky yarn with approx 92m (100yds) per 100g
- Pair of 6mm (size 10) and 7mm (size 10¹⁄₂) knitting needles or size needed to achieve tension
- Oddments of contrasting yarn
- Pony beads with added glitter
- Yarn needle

FINISHED SIZE

Hat measures 20cm (8in) deep and will fit average head. Beaded ties measure 28cm (11in) long, not including tassels.

TENSION

16 stitches and 22 rows to 10cm (4in) over stocking stitch using 6mm (size 10) needles.

KNITTING THE HAT

Knit and finish the hat following the basic pattern on page 27, changing to stocking stitch to work the rest of the hat after the first four rows of double rib have been worked.

Prefer the bag? see page 25 for the basic pattern

BEADING THE TIES

1 Mark position of ties on hat with contrasting yarn. Cut two 180cm (70in) lengths of hat yarn to make ties. Thread a length into yarn needle and thread end of yarn through hat at marked point.

2 Unthread needle and pull yarn through knitting until ends are level. Remove yarn marker and tie overhand knot in yarn close to hat edge.

3 Thread pony bead onto 1 strand of yarn and tie overhand knot in both strands below bead to secure it. Repeat until beaded tie is desired length.

4 Trim ends of yarn neatly about 2.5cm (1in) below final bead. Repeat for second tie.

fringed bag

Short beaded ties make an irregular fringe across the top of a Buttonhole Bag. Vary the lengths of the ties and attach them to the bag at random intervals, making sure you attach the centre ties below the buttonhole.

twinkle

hat with beaded brim

Add sparkle to a ribbed hat by making a narrow brim and stitching a row of pretty beads around the edge. Choose clear, silver-lined beads that go with any yarn colour or pick a contrasting colour.

YOU WILL NEED

- 2 100g balls of pure wool chunky yarn with approx 92m (100yds) per 100g
- Pair of 6mm (size 10) and 6.5mm (size 10¹⁄₂) knitting needles or size needed to achieve tension
- Silver-lined glass pebble beads
- Tapestry wool to match yarn colour
- Tapestry needle
- Yarn needle

FINISHED SIZE

Hat measures 23cm (9in) deep and will fit average head.

TENSION

16 stitches and 18 rows to 10cm (4in) over double rib, slightly stretched widthways, using 6mm (size 10) needles.

KNITTING THE HAT

Using 6.5mm (size 10¹⁄₂) needles, cast on 72 sts.

Change to 6mm (size 10) needles.

ROW 1: (RS of hat, WS of brim) Knit.

ROW 2: K1, P to last st, K1.

Rep Rows 1 & 2 once more.

Follow the basic pattern on page 27, working from Row 1 to the end.

BEADING THE BRIM

1 Cut 45cm (18in) length of tapestry or double knitting yarn and thread into tapestry needle. Secure end of yarn by weaving it up edge on wrong side of hat.

2 Bring yarn out just below first row of purl stitches on hat brim. Slot bead onto needle and slide it down yarn to rest against knitting.

3 Take needle back through knitting above same purl stitch to make vertical stitch going through bead and into knitting. Repeat along brim, applying 1 bead to every purl stitch.

4 When all beads have been applied, roll brim upwards on right side of hat so cast-on edge is aligned with first row of rib stitches. Pin in place, positioning pins vertically.

5 Using same thread as used to apply beads, stitch edge of brim neatly down onto hat, taking care to work stitches fairly loosely so edge of hat remains nice and stretchy. Join hat seam.

señorita

capelet with beaded fringe

Perfect for a party or a glamorous night out, this funky capelet is edged with a gorgeous beaded fringe. Choose lightweight beads with a metallic finish and add one or two smaller pebble beads in plain gold to some of the strands.

YOU WILL NEED

- 2 100g balls of pure wool chunky yarn with approx 92m (100yds) per 100g ball
- Pair of 6.5mm (size 10¹/₂) knitting needles or size needed to achieve tension
- Approx 220 chunky metallic beads
- Approx 60 gold pebble beads
- Matching tapestry wool
- Tapestry needle
- Yarn needle

FINISHED SIZE

Capelet measures 18cm (7in) deep and 122cm (48in) along lower edge from front to back. Ties are 38cm (15in) long.

TENSION

13 stitches and 17 rows to 10cm (4in) over stocking stitch.

KNITTING THE CAPELET

Knit and finish the capelet following the basic pattern on page 27.

Prefer the scarf? **see page 25 for the basic pattern**

MAKING THE BEADED FRINGE

1 Cut about eighty 30cm (12in) lengths of tapestry wool to make fringe. Thread 1 length into tapestry needle and insert 1 end of yarn into capelet edge.

2 Unthread needle and pull yarn through knitting until ends are level. Tie overhand knot in yarn close to capelet edge. Repeat, spacing yarn fringes evenly along edge.

3 Thread selection of 3 or 4 beads onto each yarn fringe. Thread each piece of yarn into needle and take both strands separately through beads.

4 When beads have been threaded onto both strands of yarn, tie overhand knot in yarn below beads to secure them. Repeat along lower edge of capelet. Leave yarn strands untrimmed below beads.

4

beaded scarf

Knit the basic Scarf pattern in double rib and decorate each end with a randomly beaded fringe. Knot the yarn strands in pairs as if you were making a lattice fringe (page 33), add a bead, then knot each pair of strands again below the bead. Add a smaller bead to each single strand, and knot the yarn below each one, varying the lengths of the strands to give a random effect. Trim any surplus yarn below the beads.

chapter 5

customizing knitting

So far we have shown you how you can personalize a range of accessories by **changing the edgings** and **embellishing** them with handmade or shop-bought trimmings and handles. In this chapter, you'll discover how **substituting yarns** and **stitches** can transform our five basic patterns. Try using **handspun** and **novelty** yarns, **felting** the accessories, or decorating them with simple **embroidery** stitches to stamp your own style on the pieces. By using some of the fun ideas from the earlier chapters too, you can make **one-off pieces** that are truly your own creations.

foxy

long fingerless mittens

To make these fingerless mittens, follow the basic pattern on page 26. Stop knitting before you complete both thumb and main body of the mitten and work a few rib rows before casting off. If you wish, extend the mitten cuff to fit snugly up your forearm.

1

2

YOU WILL NEED

- 2 [2, 2] 100g skeins of variegated handspun chunky yarn in 75% wool, 25% silk with approx 120m (130yds) per 100g skein
- Pair of 5mm (size 8) and 5.5mm (size 9) knitting needles or size needed to achieve tension
- Yarn needle

NOTE

When knitting with handspun yarn, you should be aware that the colour sequence in each skein will be slightly different so your pair of mittens will not be an exact match.

FINISHED SIZES

To fit women's sizes Small, Medium, Large (instructions for Medium and Large sizes are given in square brackets).

TENSION

14 stitches and 23 rows to 10cm (4in) over stocking stitch using 5.5mm (size 9) needles.

KNITTING THE MITTENS

Using 5.5mm (size 9) needles, cast on 43 [49, 55] sts.

ROW 1: (RS) K1, * P1, K1; rep from * to end.

ROW 2: * P1, K1; rep from * to last st, P1.

Rep Rows 1 & 2 once more.

Cont working in single rib, dec 1 st at each end of next and every foll 4th row until there are 29 [33, 37] sts on needle. Work 4 more rows of single rib, ending with a RS row.

NEXT ROW: Rib 6 sts, M1, (rib 4 [5, 6] sts, M1) 4 times, rib 7 sts. (34 [38, 42] sts)

Change to stocking stitch (RS rows knit, WS rows purl).

Beg with a knit row, work 4 [4, 6] rows of St st.

Follow the basic pattern from ** to ***.

NEXT ROW: P11 [13, 13], turn.

Working on these 11 [13, 13] sts only, work 0 [2, 4] rows without shaping.

Change to 5mm (size 8) needles and work 4 rows of single rib.

Cast off in rib.

With RS facing, rejoin yarn at base of thumb. Change to 5.5mm (size 9) needles and knit to end of row. (33 [35, 39] sts)

Work 5 [7, 9] rows of stocking stitch without shaping.

Change to 5mm (size 8) needles and work 4 [5, 6] rows of single rib.

Cast off in rib.

3

4

WORKING
THE MITTENS

1 Cast on number of stitches for your
size. To work arm shaping at
beginning of each decrease row, knit
first stitch, then knit next 2 stitches
together to decrease 1 stitch.

2 Work across row in single rib until you
reach last 3 stitches. Slip first stitch as
if going to knit, knit next stitch then
pass slipped stitch over knitted stitch
to decrease 1 stitch. Knit last stitch.

3 Follow pattern instructions until you
reach ***, then transfer stitches on
right needle onto waste yarn. Purl
correct number of stitches for your
size, then slip stitches on left needle
onto another piece of waste yarn.
Follow pattern instructions to complete
thumb, changing to 5mm (size 8)
needles to work rib rows.

4 To cast off thumb stitches in rib, knit
each knit stitch and purl each purl
stitch along row, casting them off in
usual way.

bella

recyled bag

Fabric strips joined together make a good yarn to knit on large needles, whether you're recycling garments or buying new yardage. Knit the basic Buttonhole Bag pattern on page 25, omitting the buttonhole, and add handles to make a very large tote. Bella has fewer stitches and rows, and so makes a smaller bag.

Tip

T-shirt fabric makes terrific bags with lots of stretch. Cut through the shirt below the sleeves to leave a tube, then cut around the tube in a spiral to make a continuous strip.

YOU WILL NEED

- Selection of plain, striped and patterned cotton fabric
- Pair of 12mm (size 17) knitting needles
- Sewing thread and sewing needle

FINISHED SIZE

Bag measures 30cm (12in) deep and 33cm (13in) wide.

TENSION

9 stitches and 14 rows to 10cm (4in) over garter stitch.

PREPARING THE YARN

Make the fabric strips as shown (right).

KNITTING THE BAG

Cast on 26 sts.

Work even in garter stitch until the front measures 30cm (12in) ending with a WS row. Cast off.

Work back to match front.

KNITTING THE HANDLES
(make two)

Cast on 7 sts. Work even in garter stitch until the handle measures 28cm (11in), ending with a WS row. Cast off.

FINISHING THE BAG

Fold the strip ends onto the wrong side and stitch to secure. Pin the handles to the wrong side of the bag pieces, overlapping the edges by about 2cm (³/₄in) and stitch them securely in place using double thread. Place the front and back together with right sides facing and stitch together with a flat seam using double thread. Turn to the right side.

PREPARING THE YARN

1 If recycling shirt fabric, cut off collars, cuffs and front bands, then trim away seams, hems and excess fabric, leaving rectangular pieces of fabric. Press all fabric.

2 Lay piece of fabric on flat surface and cut a snip in bottom edge, about 2.5cm (1 in) from right-hand side. Holding both sides of snip firmly, tear fabric upwards, stopping about 2.5cm (1in) from top edge.

3 Turn fabric over so top edge is now at bottom. Cut a snip in this edge about 2.5cm (1in) from previous tear and tear upwards, again stopping 2.5cm (1in) from fabric edge. Repeat across fabric, turning and tearing to make long continuous strip.

4 If using yardage rather than recycled fabric, tear strips in same way, but snip right across selvedges that run down edges of fabric and tear across width of fabric rather than down length.

5 Roll fabric strips into balls, joining short edges as you add new strips to ball by overlapping ends and working couple of rows of small running stitches across strips.

candy

striped scarf

Simple stripes make the basic garter stitch Scarf into something fun to snuggle into on a cold winter's day. The stripes are worked in four randomly arranged colours, so one end of the scarf looks completely different to the other end.

FUN WITH STRIPES

It's time to add some simple variations to your knitting repertoire. The easiest way to change a knit fabric is to introduce more colours. Horizontal stripes worked in two, three or more colours add zing to plain garter or stocking stitch accessories. The colour choice is down to you: stripe colours can contrast strongly or the effect can be made much more subtle by using a restricted palette of shades of one colour plus one or more co-ordinating colours. Garter stitch, stocking stitch and rib patterns all look good worked in stripes.

REPEATING STRIPES

Worked in stocking stitch, the narrow stripes are of identical widths and arranged in a repeating pattern. Work two rows in the main yarn and two rows in contrast yarn, then repeat the colour sequence.

RANDOM STRIPES

Worked in stocking stitch, these stripes are of different widths and arranged in a totally random colour sequence. Work several rows in the main yarn, then continue working in the same stitch, changing colours at random after one, two, three, or more rows have been worked.

GARTER STRIPES

The appearance of stripes worked in garter stitch varies, depending on whether the first row of the new colour starts on a right or wrong side row. On a right side row, the two yarns create a crisp line where the colour changes. On a wrong side row, the two yarns interlock to give a broken line. To make the most of this effect, change colours after an odd number of rows have been worked. The sample was worked in three-row stripes.

SEQUENCED STRIPES

Worked in double rib, the narrow stripes repeat in a different way to those in the Repeating Stripes pattern. They are arranged to give a short stripe sequence separated by bands of the main yarn. Work in the main yarn to the required point, then work: 2 rows in contrast yarn A; 2 in contrast yarn B; 8 in main yarn; 2 in contrast yarn B; 2 rows in contrast yarn A. Continue in main yarn, repeating stripe sequence as required.

jolly

rib stitch hat

This pretty hat is knit following the basic Hat pattern on page 27, but a lacy single eyelet rib is substituted for the ordinary double rib.

SINGLE EYELET RIB

This stitch pattern needs a multiple of 5 stitches plus 2.
Cast on the same number of stitches given in the basic Hat pattern
(72 = 7 x 10 + 2).

ROWS 1 & 5: (RS) P2, * K3, P2; rep from * to end.

ROWS 2, 4 & 6: K2, * P3, K2; rep from * to end.

ROW 3: P2, * K2tog, YO, K1, P2; rep from * to end.

ROW 7: P2, * K1, YO, sl 1, K1, psso, P2; rep from * to end.

ROW 8: Rep Row 2.

Rep Rows 1 to 8 for length required.

SUBSTITUTING STITCHES

Stitch patterns need a given number of stitches on the needle for the pattern to work correctly. When using a different pattern to knit a scarf, simply cast on the number required and knit a long strip. To use a different stitch to knit a shaped accessory such as a hat, you'll need to choose a stitch that works over the same number of stitches, or adjust the number by adding or subtracting one or more.

After choosing your stitch pattern, cast on the correct number and work even until you reach the point where the shaping begins.

STITCHES

You can use any of these fancy rib stitches to knit our basic Hat from page 27. The instructions include calculations for casting on the correct number of stitches for each stitch pattern.

DOUBLE EYELET RIB

This stitch pattern needs a multiple of 7 stitches plus 2.

Cast on the same number of stitches given in the basic Hat pattern (72 = 7 x 10 + 2).

ROW 1: (RS) P2, * K5, P2; rep from * to end.

ROW 2: K2, * P5, K2; rep from * to end.

ROW 3: P2, * K2tog, YO, K1, YO, sl 1, K1, psso, P2; rep from * to end.

ROW 4: Rep Row 2.

Rep Rows 1 to 4 for length required.

UNEVEN RIB

This stitch pattern needs a multiple of 4 stitches plus 3.

Cast on one stitch fewer than the number given in the basic Hat pattern (71 = 4 x 17 + 3).

ROW 1: * K2, P2; rep from * to last 3 sts, K2, P1.

Rep Row 1 for length required.

THREE-BY-ONE RIB

This stitch pattern needs a multiple of 4 stitches plus 1.

Cast on one more stitch than the number given in the basic Hat pattern (73 = 4 x 18 + 1).

ROW 1: (RS) K1, * P3, K1; rep from * to end.

ROW 2: P1, * K3, P1; rep from * to end.

Rep Rows 1 & 2 for length required.

THREE-BY-TWO RIB

This stitch pattern needs a multiple of 5 stitches plus 2.

Cast on the same number of stitches given in the basic Hat pattern (72 = 5 x 14 + 2).

ROW 1: (RS) P2, * K3, P2; rep from * to end.

ROW 2: K2, * P3, K2; rep from * to end.

Rep Rows 1 & 2 for length required.

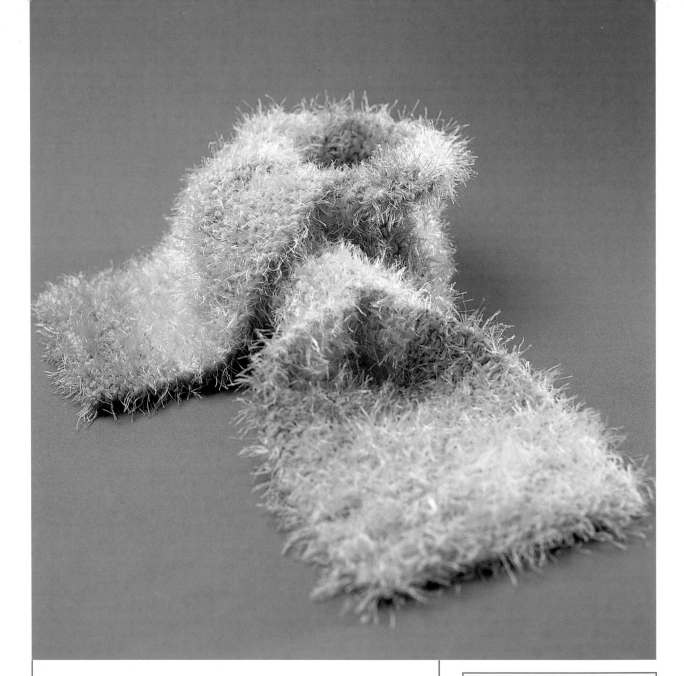

fizzy

textured scarf

Novelty yarns make fabulous scarfs that can add interest and colour to a simple outfit. This garter stitch scarf was worked from the basic Scarf pattern on page 25 using one strand of double knitting yarn in pink held together with one strand of long eyelash yarn in variegated pink, white, lilac and blue.

Tip

Novelty yarns work best with simple stitch patterns. Garter stitch makes a scarf reversible. Alternatively, knit in stocking stitch to get a different texture on the right and wrong sides of your scarf.

WORKING WITH NOVELTY YARNS

Novelty yarns come in all sorts of textures and can be a solid colour or variegated. They can be used in small amounts as decorative accents or to replace a smooth yarn when knitting a pattern, providing they work up to the same gauge.

Many novelty yarns are made from a mixture of fibres and often need special care when washing. You'll usually find the fibre composition and care details given on the ball or skein band. These yarns are a little difficult to work with because it's harder to distinguish the stitches than when knitting with smooth yarns. Concentrate and count carefully when casting on, casting off, and working increases and decreases.

The swatches shown provide an idea of the different types of novelty yarn you can buy. Each yarn is contrasted against a smooth chunky yarn made from pure wool. From top to bottom they are:

MOHAIR YARN

Mohair yarns are soft and fluffy and contain a high proportion of kid mohair spun around a synthetic core for strength. Some people find that mohair yarn feels rather itchy next to their skin. You may prefer to use it in a band to trim the ends of a scarf, knitting the body of the scarf in a non-itchy wool or cotton yarn.

EYELASH YARN

Eyelash yarn comes in many varieties, and different effects are created by the length of the 'lashes' radiating from a thin central core. This type of yarn – also called 'fun fur' – is spun from synthetic fibres. Many eyelash yarns are a similar weight to double knitting yarn. Use them double or combined with a smooth yarn of similar weight to team them with chunky weight yarns.

NOVELTY WOOLLEN YARN

Novelty yarns made from pure wool or wool/synthetic mixtures create a wide range of textures and colour combinations. Yarns may be textured with loops, bobbles and slubs or be twisted to vary from very fine to very thick at regular intervals along the yarn. The yarn in the swatch is spun from pure wool and incorporates a kaleidoscope of bright colours.

SHORT EYELASH YARN

Short eyelash yarns have a different construction from the yarns described above. A length of short eyelash yarn is made from short fibres joined at one end to form a tiny fringe. This type of yarn has a soft, velvety feel and usually has a sheen.

fjord

felted bag

These two bags were knit
from the basic Buttonhole Bag
pattern on page 25 using
Icelandic Lopi wool. The pale
blue bag was washed at 60°,
the dark blue bag was not
washed so is unfelted.

FELTING SWATCHES

Felting or – to give the process the
correct term – fulling, describes shrinking
a piece of knitted fabric so that it thickens
and becomes solid and fuzzy, yet still
pliable. Knitted felt usually shrinks more in
length than in width and the amount of
shrinkage will vary, depending on how
loosely the piece has been knitted.

The easiest way to felt something is to
machine wash it, adding an old towel or
pair of jeans to the machine for extra
friction. Pull the wet knitting gently into
shape and lay it flat to dry.

Pure wool yarns are used for felting,
but avoid those that are treated to be
machine washable, as most will not felt.
The best type to try are those wools
labelled as 'Hand Wash Only'. Some
yarns lose stitch definition quickly when
washed, while others may need several
washes before you get the effect you
want. Remember that felting is an inexact
science so always make a swatch and
wash and dry it first before starting to knit
your project. Keep on swatching until you
are happy with the results.

1 CHUNKY SHETLAND

Stocking stitch worked in two colours of chunky Shetland wool and washed on a 60º wash. The knit fabric has thickened up nicely, but there's still too much stitch definition at this stage.

2 THICK AND THIN WOOL

Stocking stitch worked in a novelty, multi-coloured thick and thin yarn and washed on a 60º wash. This yarn has felted a little bit too much, resulting in a hard, rather stiff fabric. It would be better washed at a lower temperature.

3 SHETLAND WOOL PLUS MOHAIR

Garter stitch worked in one strand of Shetland double knitting weight yarn plus one strand of mohair yarn and washed on a 60º wash. This has a lovely finish; the stitch definition is still there, but the fabric has thickened up nicely. The mohair gives the felt a soft, furry surface.

4 TWO STRANDS OF MOHAIR

Stocking stitch worked in one strand of solid colour mohair yarn plus one strand of the same yarn in a variegated colourway and washed on a 60º wash. The felt feels thick and substantial, but is still very soft.

5 ICELANDIC WOOL

Garter stitch worked in Icelandic Lopi wool and washed on a 60º wash. This type of wool felts really well, making a thick, even fabric. Dark colours may bleed during felting, so don't wash light and dark colours together.

victoria

hand-embroidered mittens

Sprinkle embroidered flowers across the back of stocking stitch Mittens for a fresh, 'country girl' look. Choose a fairly dark colour to knit the mittens, and embroider the flowers and leaves in bright shades of tapestry wool.

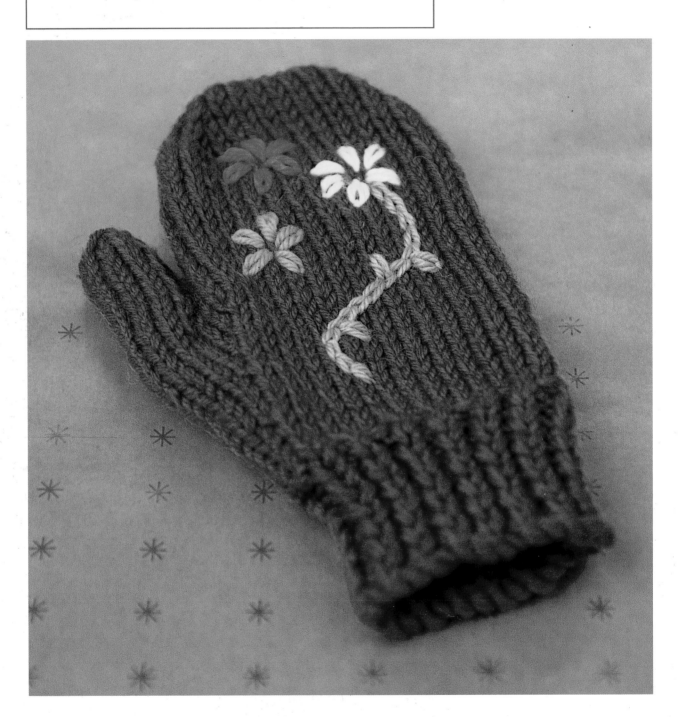

EMBROIDERY ON KNITTING

You've already learnt how to do two stitches: back stitch (page 24) and blanket stitch along an edge (page 35). Back stitch makes a good strong line when worked onto the surface of knit fabric, while blanket stitch can be worked in rows or in a circle to add decoration. Two other useful stitches are shown on these pages: chain stitch and lazy daisy stitch. Use chain stitch to work heavy lines and lazy daisy stitch to make individual flower petals. Use tapestry wool or six strands of embroidery floss to work stitches onto chunky knitting, depending on the look you want to create.

WORKING
A BLANKET STITCH ROW

1 Work blanket stitch as described on page 35, but work stitches on top of knit fabric and arrange them in a row.

WORKING CHAIN STITCH

1 Bring yarn through to right side, leaving yarn tail on surface. Take needle back through knitting close to where yarn emerged, bringing it back to right side short distance away.

2 Take working yarn under point of needle to make loop, then pull needle through to complete first stitch.

3 Repeat along row to make series of interlocking loops. At end of row, anchor last loop by making tiny straight stitch over it. Take yarn to wrong side and secure by weaving it through previous stitches. Anchor yarn tail in same way.

WORKING LAZY DAISY STITCH

1 This stitch is actually a single chain stitch. Bring needle through and make 1 chain stitch as above, then anchor loop with 1 tiny straight stitch.

2 Arrange subsequent stitches in circle to make flower shape, positioning each stitch to radiate outwards from central point. Fasten off yarn after working each flower.

chapter 6
gallery

In this section you will find all the scarfs, bags, mittens, hats and capelets made in the book. Glancing through these pages you will be able to see the many **changes** and additions that were made to the five basic patterns. Remember that the pieces shown can be made in **different colours** to suit your particular style. Take the **beads** from a hat and use them on mittens; keep the **handle** from a bag, but knit it in another yarn. We hope you'll be inspired by the gallery to mix and match elements to create your own, **completely original** accessories.

scarfs

Basic Scarf, PAGE 25

Playful, PAGE 30

Scarf with pompoms

Weekend, PAGE 32

Scarf with simple fringe

Tab, PAGE 58

Scarf with tab-and-buckle fastening (right)

Sporty, PAGE 34

Scarf with blanket-stitch edging

Tuck, PAGE 54

Scarf with slit closure

Octopus, PAGE 56

Scarf with tie ends

Swirl, PAGE 78

Scarf with beaded spirals

Firefly, PAGE 80

Scarf with knitted-in beads

Charming, PAGE 82

Scarf with charms and bells

Candy, PAGE 106

Striped scarf

Bound scarf, PAGE 39

Scarf with fabric binding

Braided scarf, PAGE 73

Scarf with braids

Fizzy, PAGE 110

Textured scarf

scarf variations

Loopy scarf, PAGE 45

Scarf with French knit edge

Slashed scarf, PAGE 88

Felted slashed scarf

Lattice scarf, PAGE 33

Scarf with knotted fringe

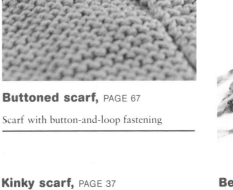

Buttoned scarf, PAGE 67

Scarf with button-and-loop fastening

Kinky scarf, PAGE 37

Scarf with curly fringe (left)

Beaded scarf, PAGE 99

Scarf with beaded fringe

bags

Basic Buttonhole Bag, PAGE 25

Curly, PAGE 36

Bag with curly fringe

Violet, PAGE 38

Felted bag with fabric binding

Honey, PAGE 64

Bag with faux tortoiseshell handles (right)

Meadow, PAGE 42

Bag with felt appliqué flowers

Kate, PAGE 60

Bag with grab handles

Susie, PAGE 62

Felted bag with drawstring handles

Flora, PAGE 84

Bag with knitted ball buttons

Pearl, PAGE 86

Bag with mother-of-pearl buttons

Jenny, PAGE 88

Slashed felted bag

Bella, PAGE 104

Recycled fabric bag

Fjord, PAGE 112

Felted bag

bag variations

Pompom bag, PAGE 31

Felted bag with pompoms

Shoulder bag, PAGE 61

Bag with shoulder strap (right)

Fluffy bag, PAGE 51

Bag with marabou trim

Knotty bag, PAGE 57

Bag with ties

Buckled bag, PAGE 59

Bag with tab-and-buckle fastening

Zipper bag, PAGE 69

Bag with zipped pocket

Buttoned bag, PAGE 71

Bag with flap and cords

Spiral bag, PAGE 79

Felted bag with beads

Fringed bag, PAGE 95

Bag with beaded fringe

mittens

Basic Mittens, PAGE 26

Zippy, PAGE 68

Shortie mittens with zip

Astra, PAGE 90

Mittens with starburst sequins

Julia, PAGE 41

Mittens with picot hem

Loopy, PAGE 66

Mittens with loop-and-button fastening

Froggy, PAGE 92

Mittens with novelty buttons

mitten variations

Dotty mittens, PAGE 43

Mittens with felt appliqué polka dots

Tasselled mittens, PAGE 49

Mittens with tassels

Foxy, PAGE 102

Long fingerless mittens

Pompom mittens, PAGE 63

Mittens with drawstring and pompoms

Victoria mittens, PAGE 114

Hand-embroidered mittens

Buttoned mittens, PAGE 84

Mittens with knitted buttons

hats

Basic Hat, PAGE 27

Paris, PAGE 44

Rib hat with French knit trim

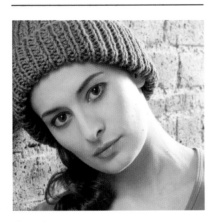

Jaunty, PAGE 46

Rib hat with turn-back cuff

Swinger, PAGE 48

Rib hat with tassel

Anna, PAGE 70

Hat with earflaps and cords

Heidi, PAGE 72

Rib hat with braided ties

Gretchen, PAGE 94

Hat with beaded ties

Twinkle, PAGE 96

Hat with beaded brim

Jolly, PAGE 108

Rib stitch hat

hat variations

Swansdown, PAGE 50

Capelet with marabou trim

Shamrock hat, PAGE 83

Hat with charms

Fishy Hat, PAGE 93

Hat with shank buttons

capelets

Bluebell, PAGE 74

Capelet with ribbon ties

Señorita, PAGE 98

Capelet with beaded fringe

Basic Capelet, PAGE 27

Index

Page numbers in italics refer to illustrations. As many of the same materials and techniques are used throughout the book, the page references are intended to direct the reader to substantial entries only.

Acknowledgments

Breslich & Foss Ltd and Jan Eaton would like to thank the following individuals for their help in the creation of this book: Nicola Hill for modelling the accessories and Jackie Jones for styling the hair and make-up; Pauline Hornsby for checking the patterns; Liz Marley for knitting many of the projects, and Martin Norris for photographing all the pieces. Last but not least, our thanks go to designer Elizabeth Healey, whose original concept this was.